D0866753

Presented To:

....

From:

....

Date:

....

Come With Me

DEVOTIONAL

A Yearlong Adventure *in* Following Jesus

Suzanne Eller

BETHANYHOUSE

a division of Baker Publishing Group
Minneapolis, Minnesota

Published by Bethany House Publishers
11400 Hampshire Avenue South
Bloomington, Minnesota 55438
www.bethanyhouse.com

Bethany House Publishers is a division of
Baker Publishing Group, Grand Rapids, Michigan

Printed in China

Library of Congress Control Number: 2017937870

ISBN 978-0-7642-1940-5

Scripture quotations identified AMP are from the Amplified® Bible, copyright
© 2015 by The Lockman Foundation. Used by permission. (www.Lockman.org)

Scripture quotations identified ESV are from The Holy Bible, English Standard
Version® (ESV®), copyright © 2001 by Crossway, a publishing ministry of Good
News Publishers. Used by permission. All rights reserved. ESV Text Edition: 2011

Scripture quotations identified GW are from *God's Word*®. © 1995 God's Word
to the Nations. Used by permission of Baker Publishing Group.

Scripture quotations identified KJV are from the King James Version of the Bible.

Scripture quotations identified NIV are from the Holy Bible, New International
Version®. NIV®. Copyright © 1973, 1978, 1984, 2011 by Biblica, Inc.™ Used by
permission of Zondervan. All rights reserved worldwide. www.zondervan.com

Scripture quotations identified NKJV are from the New King James Version®.
Copyright © 1982 by Thomas Nelson, Inc. Used by permission. All rights reserved.

Scripture quotations identified NLT are from the *Holy Bible*, New Living Translation,
copyright © 1996, 2004, 2015 by Tyndale House Foundation. Used by permission
of Tyndale House Publishers, Inc., Carol Stream, Illinois 60188. All rights reserved.

Cover design by Greg Jackson

Author is represented by The FEDD Agency

18   19   20   21   22   23   24   8   7   6   5   4   3   2

INTRODUCTION

D O YOU LONG to know Christ in a way that transforms the way you think and the way you live?

I do.

So did the early disciples. As they followed Jesus, they came to know him. That relationship shaped their faith. It changed them. Let's consider for a moment that we are walking with him in the three-plus years of his ministry here on earth.

Let's sit with him. Let's listen to his words. Let's watch as Jesus interacts with his friends and those who resist his love. Let's watch as he reaches out to people, even those who rebuff him. What would it be like to crowd in close to hear him speak and learn from him?

My prayer for this *Come With Me Devotional* is that you will walk with him as if you've never heard about him. My prayer is that you'll discover Jesus all over again.

As you read through the book of Luke, and walk with Jesus, ask these questions:

Jesus, what are you saying?
Are these words for me?
What does your example teach me?
How do I live this in my real life?

I took this personal journey nearly three years ago. I wasn't in a crisis of faith, or maybe I was. I wasn't trying to write a book. I was asking Jesus to rewrite his story on my heart. I love ministry, but somehow faith and ministry became entangled and I wanted to go back to that moment when I first encountered Jesus. When I didn't really know anything about him, or his Word.

You see, that's how the original disciples began. They had no idea what saying yes to Jesus' invitation meant. They found out as they walked with him.

Something beautiful took place as I stepped into the book of Luke and asked the questions for myself. Let me repeat those questions. They're important.

Jesus, what are you saying?
Are these words for me?
What does your example teach me?
How do I live this in my real life?

There were moments I sat with my open Bible and wept, totally lost in the beauty of what I heard or witnessed. There were times I was smack in the middle of real life, and I'd hear his words.

Not just hear them, but know where he was leading me—if only I would follow.

This is not a devotion. It's a journey of rediscovery.

Let's begin in Luke 4 as Jesus begins his public ministry. Take a seat on a craggy rock in the bleak wilderness as our Savior is led into the wilderness by the Spirit. Prepare to witness an intense battle with a real enemy as our Savior poises to rescue you and me.

Suzie

1

Filled

Then Jesus, full of the Holy Spirit, returned from the Jordan River. He was led by the Spirit in the wilderness, where he was tempted by the devil for forty days. Jesus ate nothing all that time and became very hungry.

LUKE 4:1–2 NLT

THE ENEMY CIRCLES around Jesus. He isn't after just the person, but the position of Messiah. He's poised to wage a colossal battle. He's poised to lead Jesus away from his mission.

Jesus brims with power. He walked into the wilderness filled, his Source his heavenly Father. Though this battle will last for forty long days, Jesus carries truth as his weapon and faith as his shield.

He already sees the enemy as defeated, his plans in disarray.

Let's not be surprised when the tempter seeks to distract us. Those feelings are real, but so is the power that lives on the inside.

> ## Come With Me
> *I have already won the battle. You are not battling for victory, but from a place of victory.*

Not only does Jesus understand our conflict, but the Holy Spirit rattles temptation with truth and strength. That battle we face isn't merely a person or a circumstance, but a move to distract us from our purpose.

We stand equipped, for no temptation is greater than our God.

PUSH OUT DEEPER: Luke 4:1–14; James 4:7; Hebrews 4:15; Deuteronomy 8:3

Hungry

> The devil said to him, "If you are the Son of God, tell this stone to become bread."
>
> LUKE 4:3 NIV

JESUS' STOMACH caves in with hunger. He doesn't have to be in the wilderness. With one word, the stones at Jesus' feet could be turned to bread, but he stands firm.

The adversary taunts Jesus.

You don't have to be hungry. Take things into your own hands.

Jesus faces the enemy head-on, declaring that obedience to his Father is greater than satisfying a right-now hunger.

He refuses to be deceived by one who cares less about him and more about the destruction of his soul.

We have all heard that voice of enticement. It calls us to compromise or fulfill an instant longing that takes us from the will of God.

It demands that we take things into our own hands and strip them from God's.

Come With Me

When tempted, remind the enemy—and yourself—that you are incredibly loved and made for more.

We are not alone in this battle. Our heavenly Father is aware of our needs, far beyond the right now. He will help us overcome temptation to walk into our destiny. Our Father promises to lift us above temporary desires to discover lasting transformation.

PUSH OUT DEEPER: Luke 4:3; Luke 12:31; 1 John 2:14; 1 Peter 5:8

More Than a Carpenter

"If you worship me, it will all be yours."

LUKE 4:7 NIV

A S THE TEST in the wilderness winds down, Satan has one more trick. He waves his hand over the kingdom to show Jesus lights, power, and earthly glory. He claims ownership of it all.

Perhaps he thinks the son of a carpenter will be dazzled by this offer of prominence and possessions. But Jesus is more than a carpenter's son. He's the Son of God. Nothing on earth compares to the splendor of eternity.

> **Come With Me**
> *There is nothing here on earth that compares to the treasure of what I have already given you.*

When tempted, we remind the enemy of who we are. We are adopted and grafted into the family tree as a beloved child of God.

There is no alluring display or temptation greater than our identity as his.

We were liberated by Jesus, the price his own life. We won't be drawn into slavery of any kind, for we have been redeemed and called his own.

PUSH OUT DEEPER: Luke 4:7–8; Ephesians 6:10; Galatians 4:4–5; Romans 8:16–17

4

Sent

"The Spirit of the Lord is upon me, for he has anointed me to bring Good News to the poor. He has sent me to proclaim that captives will be released, that the blind will see, that the oppressed will be set free."

LUKE 4:18 NLT

IT'S TRADITION to read the words of the law and the prophets in the synagogue. On this day Jesus takes the scrolls and reads a text from Isaiah, the prophet. The crowd is shocked at Jesus' message.

I was sent *to restore any whose spirit is impoverished and empty.*
I was sent *to release the chains of the past and words that leave a mark.*
I was sent *to open the eyes of the blind.*
I was sent *to heal the brokenhearted and put the pieces back together again.*

The crowd is unsure of Jesus' words, but sometimes we are just as unclear.

Jesus was *sent* for you and me.

When we grasp these promises as true, we are mended, unchained, loosed, and set free.

Savior, you were sent to us and we don't take that lightly. We open the door and welcome you in to every part of our broken lives. Make yourself at home in us.

> ### Come With Me
> *I was sent to, and for, you. Open your eyes to that truth, for it has the power to liberate you.*

PUSH OUT DEEPER: Luke 4:15–20; Isaiah 61:1; John 3:16–17; 2 Corinthians 3:17

You Are Wanted

Then Jesus added, "I can guarantee this truth: A prophet isn't accepted in his hometown."

LUKE 4:24 GW

JESUS SEARCHES for those who believe, and that leads him to the broken, the desperate, the spiritually empty. They cry out, "Fill me, Jesus. Open my blinded eyes. Heal my shattered soul." They clamor for his gift, while mockers and doubters in his hometown fail to welcome or appreciate him.

They presume to be well, but they are desperately sin-sick.

They pretend to have all the answers, even as they ignore that Jesus is the answer.

Jesus seeks a welcoming place to abide. What is our response? There are no high walls and no tests to pass.

We don't have to wait until we are ready, because *he* is ready.

Jesus makes himself welcome in each of us as he finds an open heart.

When we welcome him, we tell him he is wanted. We become a dwelling place for his presence and healing touch.

> ## Come With Me
> *I seek to live at home within you and make my presence known.*

PUSH OUT DEEPER: Luke 4:24–27; Romans 5:6; 1 Corinthians 3:16; Hebrews 3:6

Nail-Scarred Hands

Their city was built on a hill with a cliff. So they got up, forced Jesus out of the city, and led him to the cliff. They intended to throw him off of it. But Jesus walked right by them and went away.

LUKE 4:29–30 GW

MOMENTS EARLIER they cheered him on, but now the same crowd shoves him to a high cliff. Jesus doesn't fight back. He gently pushes through the crowd and walks away.

He doesn't try to sway them to believe.

They aren't ready to hear what he has to say, so he plants a seed in their hearts and keeps going. That seed will grow, root, and sprout, or linger for another day.

> ### Come With Me
> A person's reaction to me is a personal and spiritual battle. Ask me, and I'll give you wisdom on how to respond.

As we follow Jesus, some will listen to our message, and others will respond negatively. While few of us will be pushed to a high cliff, it's easy to plummet into discouragement, especially when the negative response comes from someone close to us.

We stay on mission and trust God, believing he loves that person even more than we do—because that is truth. Our natural instinct is to make someone see it our way, instead of letting that seed settle into her heart. Let's trust as we partner with the Holy Spirit. Let's talk to God about that person as we wait and place her in Jesus' nail-scarred hands. As we do, the Holy Spirit works behind the scenes in spectacular ways.

PUSH OUT DEEPER: Luke 4:28–30; Mark 1:38; 2 Corinthians 3:3; James 5:16

Muzzled

"Go away! Why are you interfering with us, Jesus of Nazareth?
Have you come to destroy us? I know who you are—the Holy
One of God!"

LUKE 4:34 NLT

JESUS IS TEACHING in Capernaum when a man leaps to his feet and
screams. He's tormented by demons and runs to Jesus, declaring that
Jesus is the Holy One.

Jesus sees through the chaos to the man and muzzles the brokenness
within. Moments later, the man stands at peace and in his right mind.
Nothing is too great for our Lord!

Anxious feelings storm in, and torment attempts to take root. The noise is loud in our ears
and thunders in our soul. Jesus doesn't shy away
from the depths of our angst. He looks beyond
our outward symptoms to see us individually.

He muzzles our disquieting thoughts and stills
our minds.

> **Come With Me**
> *The fact that you*
> *struggle with anxious*
> *thoughts doesn't push*
> *me away. I long to settle*
> *your heart with peace.*

Jesus, speak to our hurting places and calm our thoughts. Take our
anxious souls and produce utter peace.

PUSH OUT DEEPER: Luke 4:33–35; Luke 8:27; Luke 8:1–3; 2 Thessalonians 3:16

All Day Long

> At sunset, the people brought to Jesus all who had various kinds
> of sickness, and laying his hands on each one, he healed them.
>
> LUKE 4:40 NIV

SIMON PETER'S MOTHER-IN-LAW is desperately sick. This is no ordinary fever; it could rob her of life. Jesus places his hands on the woman and rebukes the sickness, demanding it leave her body. She climbs from bed, from near death to life! News of the miracle flies through the town as if on wings.

People flock to Jesus in great numbers, and he prays.

And he prays. And he prays some more.

Even as the dying embers of the sun slip away, Jesus remains until the last person has been seen. This is our Jesus! He intentionally placed his feet on a passage to love and mend humanity. Compassion compelled him to bear the weight of our sin on the cross. He cares about sickness, whether in body or spirit.

> ### Come With Me
> *When you are struggling in body, mind, or soul, whisper my name.*

We are invited to call out to our great Physician. He places his hands on those we love. We show him our work-in-progress places, and he is our remedy. There's no timetable in healing. There's no rush. Jesus lingers with us from the moment we call his name. He's with us in every part of the battle, from the beginning all the way through to the end.

PUSH OUT DEEPER: Luke 4:33–41; Jeremiah 32:17; Hebrews 13:8; Psalm 59:16

Bottom of Empty

In the morning he went to a place where he could be alone. The crowds searched for him. When they came to him, they tried to keep him from leaving.

LUKE 4:42 GW

JESUS' COUSIN, John, lingers in prison. His fate is uncertain, and that weighs heavily on the Master. He's been with the crowds all day long. Finally, he slips away. Just as Jesus has poured out, he intentionally fills back up as he talks with his heavenly Father.

We don't need to live on empty.

Cares and concerns weigh heavy. We don't have all the answers. We continue to pour out and pour out, because that's what we do. We give ourselves in ministry, in our jobs, in our roles as sons, daughters, friends, parents, spouses, and we become empty.

Time out from people and time alone with God renews our strength.

It alters our attitude. It allows us to love and serve from a place of rest, rather than pouring out from an unfilled vessel.

> ### Come With Me
> *Pour in as much as you pour out, my beloved. It won't feel familiar at first, but soon you'll see the beauty.*

Is that jar empty? Let's take it to Jesus, for he graciously promises to fill us back up.

PUSH OUT DEEPER: Luke 4:42; Jeremiah 17:8; Jeremiah 31:25; Psalm 91:1

— 10 —

He's in Your Boat

So Jesus got into the boat that belonged to Simon and asked him
to push off a little from the shore.

LUKE 5:3 GW

AFTER CLEANING THEM, Simon Peter lugs the heavy nets back to the boat. There he finds Jesus perched inside. The fishing vessel is a perfect floating platform for Jesus to speak to the crowds.

This isn't Simon's first meeting with Jesus. They met when Andrew, Simon Peter's brother, introduced them on the shore. It was a memorable day. Jesus called Simon a Rock. They followed him that day, but here he is back to the same old fishing scene. Jesus knew exactly where to find him.

> **Come With Me**
> *You are never so far that I stop seeking you.*

We may believe we've stumbled too far from where we first met Jesus. Yet here he is, perched in our "boat." He knows where to find us—right in that situation, right where we are.

He calls us to walk back into the deep to reexperience who he is and rediscover who we are.

Jesus, thank you for perching in our boat, wherever that might be, and calling us one more time to follow you.

PUSH OUT DEEPER: Luke 5:1–3; Matthew 4:18–20; Luke 15:8–9; Ezekiel 34:12

11

Waiting

Then he sat down and taught the people from the boat.

LUKE 5:3 NIV

THE WEATHERED BOAT is Simon's livelihood and he can't leave it, so he waits.

Waiting is rarely the comfortable option. Waiting for Jesus can feel even harder. When we are expecting an answer to prayer, we want to hear a solution now. When we are anticipating a particular timing, we itch for a plan. When these fail to arrive quickly, we may give up and try to make them happen in our own power or our own timing.

Waiting is not an idle part of our walk with Jesus.

For some of us, it's a time of rest. For others, he's asking that we pause long enough to clearly hear his instructions.

Come With Me
Let me show you what I have for you in this time of waiting.

When we are in a season of waiting, let's take our eyes off the finish line. We are on his heart. He is aware of where we are.

Waiting is never wasted, and it just might be where God's greatest work takes place in us.

PUSH OUT DEEPER: Luke 5:4–7; Psalm 130:5; Micah 7:7; Isaiah 40:31

12
One More Time

When He had finished speaking, He said to Simon [Peter], "Put out into the deep water and lower your nets for a catch [of fish]."

LUKE 5:4 AMP

SIMON RESISTS putting his nets into the water with good reason. He has fished all night. He has salt on his cheeks, and the sun has burned his arms brown since he was a child.

Fishing is what he does for a living; it's what he knows. Jesus is a teacher, perhaps a rabbi, but definitely not a fisherman. Simon Peter is the expert. Or is he?

We may ask the same question. Following Jesus' instructions isn't in our natural bent. It's difficult to be asked to try one more time when we've already tried and seemingly failed. It's difficult when we are tired and God asks us to go deeper.

We may even argue that we are the experts of our own lives.

God sees what we don't. When he asks Simon to fish one more time, he sees below the waterline. It is less about the fish and more about walking into the deep. If He asks us to throw out our nets one more time—whatever that might look like—there's a reason.

Jesus, we don't see your plan, but we trust you. Today we whisper *yes* where *no* wants to take root.

> ### Come With Me
> *When you push into the deep one more time, I will meet you there.*

PUSH OUT DEEPER: Luke 5:4–7; John 15:4; 2 Corinthians 12:9; 1 Corinthians 2:5

13

Awe

When Simon Peter realized what had happened, he fell to his knees before Jesus and said, "Oh, Lord, please leave me—I'm such a sinful man." For he was awestruck by the number of fish they had caught, as were the others with him.

LUKE 5:8–9 NLT

A S THE FISH flop and overflow in the nets, Simon sees Jesus clearly for the first time. The man sitting in his boat is more than a teacher!

He is the Messiah!

That thrusts Simon into a dilemma. He suddenly sees his humanity in light of the miracle. He cries out for Jesus to leave him, but it's not in terror.

It's out of a sense of his own unworthiness.

When we compare our human limitations to Jesus' greatness, we might be tempted to hide or turn away from his presence. Instead of retreating, let's kneel in awe. Let's open our hearts to the possibilities of knowing him as Lord.

> **Come With Me**
> *You may feel tempted to turn away from me. Turn toward me instead.*

Our faith *in* him leads us closer to him.

When our human nature attempts to lead us away in fear or shame, we look to him with expectation instead.

PUSH OUT DEEPER: Luke 5:8–16; Psalm 18:6; Colossians 2:2–3; Ephesians 3:16–19

People Catcher

> Jesus told Simon, "Don't be afraid. From now on you will catch people instead of fish."
>
> LUKE 5:10 GW

SIMON PAYS HIS BILLS by catching fish, but Jesus has another vocation for him. Rather than lugging nets through the sea for fish, he will pray for the lame and they will walk in Jesus' name. Simon Peter will speak to multitudes and they'll be saved.

People will be drawn to the gospel and made alive!

Like Simon Peter, we have a job. We are people catchers. No matter where we work, our ministry is to draw people as close to Jesus as we can. When we are fearful of what this looks like, the Holy Spirit reveals what to do. He'll show us the right words to speak, and what that looks like as we live as "catchers of men."

> **Come With Me**
>
> *Ministry isn't limited to a church building, for all who believe are my church.*

The weight of saving the world isn't on our shoulders. That's his job. All we are asked to do is to be aware of those he places in our path.

Father, show us that one who doesn't know you love him. Thank you for the words to say in the right season.

PUSH OUT DEEPER: Luke 5:8–11; Luke 12:12; Matthew 10:20; Acts 1:8

The Real Miracle

> So they pulled their boats up on shore, left everything and fol-
> lowed him.
>
> LUKE 5:11 NIV

SIMON PETER doesn't build a shrine to the heap of fish. He doesn't boast about the miracle. He strides into step beside Jesus, and off he goes, leaving the fish behind.

The pile of fish was never the real miracle. It was the discovery of Jesus. Simon Peter walked into the deep and came out a changed man with a new name.

Our greatest miracle isn't what we do or how much we accomplish. It's walking with Jesus in the deep. If we are fortunate enough to enjoy success or recognition, or to accumulate material goods, all of these hold far less value than our relationship with him.

Our "fish" do not define us, even as society shouts out that they do.

Everything we own, everything we have—it's all his to do with as he desires.

As long as we have Jesus, we are blessed.

> **Come With Me**
> *Your success, or lack of it, doesn't describe your value to me. Your obedience and faith are your finest story.*

PUSH OUT DEEPER: Luke 5:10–11; Matthew 19:29; Philippians 3:7–8; Hebrews 11:26

Clean

> One day Jesus was in a city where there was a man covered with a serious skin disease. When the man saw Jesus, he bowed with his face to the ground. He begged Jesus, "Sir, if you want to, you can make me clean."
>
> LUKE 5:12 GW

A PERSON WHO SUFFERS with a skin disease is considered unclean, and leprosy is one of the most dreaded. Lepers are unwelcome in a neighbor's home or at the temple. They are not seen for their personality or virtue, but by their external condition only. When Jesus puts his hands on the leper, it is scandalous.

It makes Jesus unclean, at least in the opinion of those watching.

The leper's unclean state did not taint Jesus. Instead, Jesus' holiness made the leper clean!

Regardless of the conditions that push some away, Jesus comes close. He reaches to touch, whether our condition is skin-deep, where all can see, or hidden in the secret places in our heart. With Jesus, we are more than an obvious condition. We are created in his image. One touch and we are cleansed and made whole.

Come With Me

Those things that push others away do not keep me at a distance.

Jesus, help us see people more than skin-deep. Help us see them as you do.

PUSH OUT DEEPER: Luke 5:12–16; Leviticus 14:30–32; 2 Corinthians 5:21; Romans 8:3

17

Don't Tell Anyone

> Then Jesus ordered him, "Don't tell anyone, but go, show yourself
> to the priest and offer the sacrifices that Moses commanded for
> your cleansing, as a testimony to them."
>
> LUKE 5:14 NIV

THE FORGOTTEN SENSATION of human contact reminds the leper that he is alive. His skin is brand-new. He is free to return to his family! He will sit among his neighbors in the synagogue and hold his children on his lap.

He can walk in the marketplace and hold a job.

His life is changed for the better.

Why would Jesus ask him to keep such good news to himself? The word will spread quickly enough as neighbors and family view the leper's healed condition. The local priest will be stunned when the leper walks through the gate, laughing, holding up hands with the skin of a new baby.

His handiwork is highlighted in us. Our testimony shines through uncontained joy. His healing power spills out with every word we share. As we live healed and whole, no one can deny who God is or what he has done.

> **Come With Me**
> *Your healing leads others to me. Tell your story to someone today.*

PUSH OUT DEEPER: Luke 5:14; Luke 10:2; 1 Peter 4:11; Romans 11:36

People, People, Everywhere

But he would withdraw to desolate places and pray.

LUKE 5:16 ESV

MEN, WOMEN, AND CHILDREN witness the healed leper walking their streets. They run to their homes. They grab the sick. They tell their friends and gather to see what happens next.

Jesus looks over the scene. It's filled with people, people, and more people. After a long day he withdraws to pray. The words shared between Jesus and his heavenly Father aren't heard, but he is strengthened in the encounter.

> **Come With Me**
>
> *I love those to whom you minister, but I love you just as much. Find that alone place with me, and I'll soothe your tired soul.*

Praying is not just a tradition. It's untapped power. It's untapped revolution. It's untapped transformation. When we are honest with our heavenly Father, we find refreshment from pressing needs. It's our sanctuary where we can be ourselves. Prayer is where God steps into our weary souls and rains wisdom and replenishment. We are equipped and refreshed, and our tired hearts are renewed.

Father, when we are weary, we tend to keep on going. But there's nothing more important than you. Remind us of the power of prayer, not just over the lives of others but over our own lives.

PUSH OUT DEEPER: Luke 5:15–16; Luke 9:29; Psalm 142:2; Hebrews 4:16

Scallywags

> One day while Jesus was teaching, some Pharisees and teachers of
> religious law were sitting nearby. (It seemed that these men showed
> up from every village in all Galilee and Judea, as well as from Je-
> rusalem.) And the Lord's healing power was strongly with Jesus.
>
> LUKE 5:17 NLT

LIKE AN UNWELCOME ITCH, religious rulers and scribes shadow
Jesus' every move. They come from Galilee, Judea, and Jerusalem.
They aren't drawn by his power, but by the threat to their own.

Every time Jesus speaks, it is to a mixed crowd. He teaches to those
who adore him and to those who need his help.
He preaches to those who are intrigued and to
those who question and mock his every move.

He doesn't seek a crowd of fans.

He shares the gospel with all who listen, even
the scallywags.

As we do his work, we will encounter a mix of
people. It is frustrating when difficult people are
in the mix because it's far easier to love those who
love us back. Like Jesus, we are defined not by who is in the crowd, but
by the power of God working in us as we love those people in his name.

Come With Me
*Some who seem the
most difficult are the
most broken, and their
actions reflect that
brokenness. Reflect
me in your response.*

PUSH OUT DEEPER: Luke 5:17; Mark 1:45; Matthew 5:16; 1 Peter 2:12

Let Me Carry You

Some men brought a paralyzed man on a stretcher. They tried to take him into the house and put him in front of Jesus. But they could not find a way to get him into the house because of the crowd. So they went up on the roof. They made an opening in the tiles and let the man down on his stretcher among the people. (They lowered him in front of Jesus.)

LUKE 5:18–19 GW

A HANDFUL OF FRIENDS tote their paralyzed friend through jammed streets. As hard as they try, they can't get close to the teacher. In desperation they climb up on the roof, remove clay tiles, and let down their friend through the narrow opening. Their friend lands directly in front of Jesus. Within moments he stands to his feet and walks away!

When a friend's situation seems dire, we might not know what to do.

Let's carry that friend to Jesus. We don't have to have the right words. We don't have to fix her situation. When we sit with a friend, she is reminded that she is not isolated. When we pray with her, it reaches heaven even when there are no words.

Let's tell a friend she is worth fighting for. We aren't asked to fix her, but to bring her as close to Jesus as we can.

> ### Come With Me
> *When a friend feels like the world is tumbling down, be near to her. Your presence is a reminder of mine.*

PUSH OUT DEEPER: Luke 5:18–25; John 13:34; Ephesians 5:2; Hebrews 13:1

God Alone

> The Pharisees and the teachers of the law began thinking to themselves, "Who is this fellow who speaks blasphemy? Who can forgive sins but God alone?"
>
> LUKE 5:21 NIV

WHEN JESUS FORGIVES the paralyzed man's sins, the crowd is confused. The man's legs are the obvious problem, not his soul. Some declare Jesus' words as blasphemous. Only God can say these things! They fail to realize Jesus is the Son of God. He's keenly aware of the man's outer infirmities, but he probes deeper to the man's heart. It would be a shame to rise from a mat healed on the outside but still a mess on the inside.

There are times we are like those people in the crowd. We home in on obvious issues—anger, struggles, addiction—while Jesus seeks to address the cause of the pain. He probes beneath the exterior to do healing work in the hidden regions of their hearts.

> **Come With Me**
> *I want to heal the obvious problem, but there's more that I see. I want to heal all of you.*

He does that for others, and it's his promise for each of us as well.

Jesus, show us what is under the surface. It's not ours to fix, but we desire compassion so that we can pray.

PUSH OUT DEEPER: Luke 5:20–26; 2 Corinthians 3:17; Psalm 139:1; Jeremiah 17:4

Unlikely

Later, as Jesus left the town, he saw a tax collector named Levi sitting at his tax collector's booth. "Follow me and be my disciple," Jesus said to him.

LUKE 5:27–28 NLT

MATTHEW, ALSO KNOWN AS LEVI, COLLECTS TOLLS near Capernaum. His job as a tax collector is one of hard-nosed authority. He's feared, as many tax collectors are. Many publicans cushion their earnings with illegal tolls and unjust taxation.

What makes it worse is that Matthew is a Levite. He is destined to serve the people, not rob them.

Jesus stops before him when most of his own people go out of the way to avoid him. While others see a lost cause, Jesus sees a lost man. Matthew leaves his post as toll collector and follows Jesus, leaving behind wealth, position, and power.

> **Come With Me**
> *I don't see a lost cause; I see someone in need of a miracle.*

He's exchanging a bank account for riches that cannot be taken from him. He's exchanging power for authority that only Christ can give.

Many have misplaced their identity. They are far from home. No person is so lost that Jesus doesn't seek them. No place is so far that Jesus cannot help them find their way back.

Savior, there are days we feel far from home and beat ourselves up for the error of our ways. You know us. Thank you for leading us home.

PUSH OUT DEEPER: Luke 5:27–28; Luke 5:11; Mark 10:29; Luke 8:8

Tell Someone

And Levi made him a great feast in his house, and there was a large company of tax collectors and others reclining at table with them.

LUKE 5:29 ESV

MATTHEW SENDS OUT HIS SERVANTS to call in all of his friends for a feast. The house fills up wall to wall. Jesus is the guest of honor in a house overrunning with publicans and sinners.

Matthew's friends can't help but notice that something is different. He's free. He's joy-filled.

Might it have something to do with Jesus?

Matthew's first move as a believer is to invite others to meet Jesus, yet our society tells us to keep our faith quiet. Not everyone wants to hear, but there are many seeking him.

How will they find him if we hold back such good news?

> ### Come With Me
> *I'll show you someone who longs to know me. It may surprise you how close they are.*

Faith is a life-giving gift. Let's invite those who don't know Jesus around the table to unwrap this precious gift for themselves.

PUSH OUT DEEPER: Luke 5:28–30; 2 Timothy 1:8; Romans 1:16; Psalm 119:46

When Our Good Is Bad

> But the Pharisees and their teachers of religious law complained bitterly to Jesus' disciples, "Why do you eat and drink with such scum?"
>
> LUKE 5:30 NLT

THE RELIGIOUS GUYS stand close to the courtyard but don't dare go inside. If they sit around the table with *scum*, it will mark them as a friend of sinners.

It's a line they refuse to cross.

They are furious to the point of red-faced fits and complain bitterly.

They rant about the publicans' badness, failing to see that their "goodness" is just as great a barrier to a relationship with God.

When our faith becomes about how holy we are, we elevate ourselves rather than God.

We have all sinned and fall short.

Our goodness pales in comparison to the cross.

We all fall short of perfection.

Our goodness is found only in the truth that Jesus is a friend of sinners, and we were once lost in sin. He shows us new mercy every single day.

> ## Come With Me
> My relationship with you is not defined by how far you fall short, but by how far I reached to find you in the first place.

PUSH OUT DEEPER: Luke 5:29–31; Romans 3:23; Philippians 4:9; Psalm 51:12

Light Bearer

Jesus answered them, "Healthy people don't need a doctor—sick people do."

LUKE 5:31 NLT

JESUS IS A RULE BREAKER, but not a troublemaker. He exposes social rules that don't make sense. He isn't interested in rebellion, but in doing the work of his Father. When he sits at Matthew's table, it is to represent his Father. His conversation isn't compromised. His affection for those around the table is genuine. He isn't worried about being infected with sin, but desires to bring medicine to those who are sick.

Our faith will guide us to those who don't know Jesus as their Savior.

In those moments we are light bearers. We go where Jesus leads. Sometimes that leads us to confront sin on others' behalf in prayer.

Sometimes Jesus takes us to those sinners whom others might not condone.

> ### Come With Me
> *Everywhere you go, I am with you. Bring my light into every place, no matter how dark it may seem.*

As we invite them to come close to Jesus, we bring Jesus with us. Our words and actions reflect who he is, no matter where we are. As Jesus leads us to the highways and byways, he has the seat of honor as we dine with those who don't know him.

PUSH OUT DEEPER: Luke 5:31–32; Luke 4:18–19; Luke 15:7; Matthew 18:11

Brand-New!

"And no one puts new wine into old wineskins; or else the new
wine will burst the wineskins and be spilled, and the wineskins
will be ruined."

LUKE 5:37 NKJV

WHEN WINE IS FERMENTED, it's safe to put it in any container.
If it's in the process of fermenting, however, it will expand and
burst in a bottle or old wineskin.

Tongue in cheek, Jesus describes the Pharisees.

They are comfortable with tradition and steadfastly hold on to their
old way of thinking. Jesus longs to give them the new, but they resist.
If "new wine" is put in "old wineskins," they'll burst because they aren't
ready.

Come With Me
*Do you feel the new
I'm creating in
you? Embrace it.*

As we walk with Jesus, he shows us a new
way to think. He asks us to believe big when we
are used to dreaming small. He asks that we see
ourselves in a·new way. He takes us in a new
direction.

Can we be honest?

Clinging to the old feels less challenging and much less awkward.
But if we cling to the old, we are stuck. God desires to do a new work
in every believer.

Jesus, today we release the old and stride into the new you have
waiting for us.

PUSH OUT DEEPER: Luke 5:36–39; 2 Corinthians 5:17; Isaiah 43:19; Hebrews 8:13

Nitpicky Faith

One Sabbath Jesus was going through the grainfields, and his
disciples began to pick some heads of grain, rub them in their
hands and eat the kernels.

LUKE 6:1 NIV

DISCIPLES RUB CORN between their hands until the kernels break loose and then eat them. The Pharisees confront Jesus, demanding to know if he is aware that the disciples are breaking the law.

Jesus understands the law well. So do the Pharisees, at least their version. They have dissected and distorted it, heaping additional rules until the law is an unwieldy burden. No one can follow all of their rules.

Sadly, they have missed God's original intention and created nitpicky faith. They miss the beauty of God's direction and make certain that everyone else does too.

> **Come With Me**
> *Don't allow manmade
> rules to keep you
> far from me.*

Jesus came to set us free, not tie us up.

What rules keep us at a distance? Let's examine those. Are they biblical or manmade? His mission has always been to draw us close to the Father. We come close to him as we love him with all of our hearts, and as we love one another. His commandments are simple. When we follow these, we follow Jesus.

PUSH OUT DEEPER: Luke 6:1–5; John 1:1; John 1:14; Hebrews 4:12

Mercy Moments

He looked around at them all, and then said to the man, "Stretch out your hand." He did so, and his hand was completely restored.

LUKE 6:10 NIV

HIS HAND is withered and useless. It's a painful condition, and the religious rulers know Jesus won't miss an opportunity to show mercy. They've followed him long enough to know his character. Just as they anticipate, Jesus eases the man's suffering. They explode in anger. They are so tuned in to their own rules that they miss the gift of mercy.

Every day we run into mercy moments.

People disappoint us. They break a rule that is important. They say the wrong thing. They don't measure up. They don't do things our way.

Sometimes that person is us. We are disappointed in ourselves. We wish we'd done better or differently.

Rules are important, but so is mercy.

There is no agenda greater than the child or person standing in front of us, or looking back in the mirror. Mercy is more than a second chance; it's reminding that person she is worthy of a second chance.

Come With Me

You've experienced mercy. Take a measure of that mercy and pour it over someone else, even if that is you.

PUSH OUT DEEPER: Luke 6:6–11; 1 Timothy 1:16; Ephesians 2:4–5; Ephesians 2:7

Roar

> But they were filled with rage, and discussed with one another
> what they might do to Jesus.
>
> LUKE 6:11 NKJV

ONE DAY THERE is a roar of applause. The next there are roars of anger. Jesus' popularity rises and falls. The sounds in his ears are deafening, whether flattery or condemnation.

Jesus tunes in to one voice only.

Sometimes the roar in our ears makes it hard to think. Criticism makes us doubt ourselves. Applause may cause us to think more of ourselves than we should. Those roars feel like a *tap-tap-tap* that won't go away.

They hold far less weight than the words of our heavenly Father.

Our God has no agenda. His words do not rise or plummet based on feeling. He's not offering his opinion, but words that are certain and spot-on, based on his knowledge of who we are.

> ### Come With Me
> *Silence is a learned art.*
> *It won't come naturally.*
> *Shut down the noise*
> *until the silence allows*
> *my voice to emerge.*

There will always be a roar. It loses its influence when we listen only to Jesus. We aren't flung to the right or the left by the noise of the crowd. When the roar overwhelms, we shut it out to hear his voice.

PUSH OUT DEEPER: Luke 6:10–11; 2 Thessalonians 3:16; John 14:27; Philippians 4:7

Wisdom

And when day came, he called his disciples and chose from them
twelve, whom he named apostles.

LUKE 6:13 ESV

THE NEWLY APPOINTED DISCIPLES have strengths, but also weaknesses. They'll be refined as they walk with Jesus, but none of them have done anything like this before. That's apparent from the first day.

In the natural, most of them don't seem like the right choice. They are far from perfect. Some are unschooled. Others are uncouth. Yet Jesus prayed all night to find the right people for his team.

When he announced their names, his voice rang out clear: "Simon, Andrew, James, John . . ." It was with the knowledge that this was God's will.

> **Come With Me**
> As you make difficult leadership decisions, let me show you what you might not see.

Leading others is a challenge. Picking a team is complex. It's wise to seek earthly counsel, but our first leadership decision is to pray. God knows the heart of each person under consideration. He may point out an unlikely choice, but he sees beyond the rough edges. For leaders, there are always decisions to be made. Prayer is our first and strongest choice.

Father, thank you for allowing us to lead. Remind us not to do it in our power. You are the most valuable member of the team.

PUSH OUT DEEPER: Luke 6:12–16; 2 Samuel 24:12; Proverbs 2:10; Proverbs 6:22

Chosen

Simon, whom He named Peter, and Andrew his brother, and James
and John, and Philip, and Bartholomew, and Matthew, and Thomas,
James the son of Alphaeus, and Simon who was called the Zealot,
and Judas the son of James, and Judas Iscariot, who became a traitor.

LUKE 6:14–16 ESV

DOES JESUS REALIZE James's and John's tempers will flare at
inconvenient times? Does he know Peter will betray him?

He does. He also knows they will learn. James and John will discover
that a gentle response is the best answer. Peter will betray him, but go
on to win thousands to Christ.

Jesus chose each disciple in spite of his shortcomings. Each had a part to play.

We are chosen.

He chose us when we were a work in progress.
He chose us in spite of our weaknesses. There will
be times we succeed, and that's awesome. There

> ## Come With Me
> *Failure tempts you to
> give up. Surrender to
> me when you fail.*

will be times we fail, and that's when our choice springs into action.

We choose *him.*

We choose his forgiveness on the days we fall short. We choose to sit
at his feet and grow in our understanding. We choose to learn through
our errors.

We choose Jesus every day, for his strength is greater than our
strengths and our shortcomings.

PUSH OUT DEEPER: Luke 6:14–16; John 13:12; Jeremiah 1:5; 1 Peter 2:9

Power

Everyone tried to touch him, because healing power went out from him, and he healed everyone.

LUKE 6:19 NLT

THE DUSTY WRITINGS of Isaiah the prophet have come to life for the Twelve.

This *is* the Messiah!

Every word the teacher speaks draws them closer to this conclusion. Every time he prays for someone and they walk away renewed, it confirms their beliefs. They see the healing power in Jesus.

The longer they walk with him, the more they discover that Jesus is Lord.

He is the Messiah!

When someone asks us to tell about our faith, we have a story to share. We prayed and felt his presence. We searched for him and found that he was close. We asked for wisdom and it was granted.

> ## Come With Me
> *I'm not asking you to be me, but to allow my power to work through you.*

God is powerful.

As we share our story, that power reaches farther than we can imagine.

PUSH OUT DEEPER: Luke 6:17–19; Romans 10:14–15; Isaiah 40:9; Matthew 5:2

Blessing

"Blessed are you when people hate you, avoid you, insult you, and slander you because you are committed to the Son of Man. Rejoice then, and be very happy! You have a great reward in heaven. That's the way their ancestors treated the prophets."

LUKE 6:22–23 GW

JESUS AND HIS TWELVE newly chosen disciples come down from the mountain. They stand shoulder to shoulder with Jesus as he preaches an astounding sermon.

Blessed are you when people hate you.

Simon the Zealot is among the disciples. He surely struggles. As a Zealot, he wars against those who insult him, rather than turn the other cheek. As a Zealot, he can't imagine finding a blessing in loving his oppressor. Simon is a zealous man, but his zeal turns to passion for Christ.

Over time, that changes his battle strategy.

What is our battle strategy? Flesh says retaliate, while faith says forgive. Flesh demands retribution, while faith leads to just action. Our battle is greater than flesh and blood. We are warring against principalities and powers. The real enemy is confounded as we respond in love.

We are blessed as we choose a restored heart over revenge, and resolution over trying to prove our point.

> ### Come With Me
> *Your identity isn't founded in the words of a broken person. Don't embrace them as truth.*

PUSH OUT DEEPER: Luke 6:21–23; Luke 9:23; 2 Corinthians 12:10; Romans 8:35

Woe

> "What sorrow awaits you who are rich, for you have your only happiness now. What sorrow awaits you who are fat and prosperous now, for a time of awful hunger awaits you. What sorrow awaits you who laugh now, for your laughing will turn to mourning and sorrow."
>
> LUKE 6:24–25 NLT

IS BLESSING FOUND only in suffering?

Is it wrong to laugh?

If a person is blessed financially, is that wrong?

That's not what Jesus is saying at all. He's reminding his audience that security that comes from these things is not enough to sustain anyone.

It's great to be in good company, but it's who we are when we are alone that defines our character.

Prosperity is a luxury, but it will never feed our souls.

> ### Come With Me
> *Hold things lightly, so that you will find joy in what lasts forever.*

Jesus leads us to joy that is eternal and long lasting. Money and material goods take care of our needs, but there is pleasure in blessing others. Laughter is good for the soul, but something beautiful takes place when we cause another to smile. Our happiness will never be rooted in things or money or fleeting feelings. Our blessings are a priceless reflection of the Source within.

PUSH OUT DEEPER: Luke 6:24–26; Psalm 62:2; Matthew 7:24–27; Galatians 5:1

The Law of Love

> "Do for other people everything you want them to do for you. If you love those who love you, do you deserve any thanks for that? Even sinners love those who love them."
>
> LUKE 6:31–32 GW

PROPHETS OF OLD spoke in the presence of kings and powerful religious rulers. They heard from God and acted, even when it angered their listeners. Their faithfulness changed nations. As the disciples stand on the precipice of their mission, they will experience injustice, just as the prophets did. They will speak and listeners won't be prepared to hear what they have to say. They'll be mocked. They'll be run out of town.

The law of love will serve them well: Do for other people what you want them to do for you.

What if we made it to the end of our lives having only loved those who loved us back?

Treating people the way we want to be treated is a strong move on our part. We refuse to back away from confronting prejudice or wrongdoing, and act right in our response.

> ### Come With Me
> *When unsure of how to respond, give that person what you would hope to receive in the same situation.*

We refuse to step on people to get our way.

The law of God's love becomes an identifying mark on our lives, as we give to others what we need so desperately for ourselves.

PUSH OUT DEEPER: Luke 6:27–36; James 2:8; 1 Peter 2:19; 1 John 4:10

Degree of Mercy

"Be merciful, even as your Father is merciful."

LUKE 6:36 ESV

WHO WANTS TO SHOW MERCY to someone who slaps you on your cheek? Who would willingly give away their tunic even as their cloak is demanded? Who gives all of their treasure to someone who offers no gratitude in return?

Jesus did.

He was beaten and bruised and hung upon a rugged tree. He was stripped of his dignity and his clothing. So great was his sacrifice that God above turned away at the sight. Jesus was afflicted with our sin wounds, yet he remains merciful to each of us. We are washed clean. We are invited to come boldly into his presence when all we feel is shame. We emerge from that meeting bathed in his kindness, repaired and reinstated!

> ### Come With Me
> *My mercy is poured out over your life every single day. What degree of mercy will you give to another?*

When we receive that gift for ourselves but withhold it from others, we demean such a precious gift.

Let's remember God's compassion toward us. Let's offer a degree of mercy from that deep well.

Rather than count the wrongs of others, we will number all the times God has loved us with a merciful heart.

PUSH OUT DEEPER: Luke 6:27–36; Matthew 27:35; Titus 3:5; John 19:2

Eye for an Eye

"Judge not, and you shall not be judged. Condemn not, and you shall not be condemned. Forgive, and you will be forgiven."

LUKE 6:37 NKJV

EVERY OFFENSE is tallied in this eye-for-an-eye culture. Revenge is greater than reconciliation. Digging for evidence is greater than mediation. Many citizens go to court instead of working through the problem with their neighbor. It's into this chaotic culture that Jesus spoke.

Judge not and you shall not be judged.

Don't be so quick to condemn.

Forgive because there might be a time when you need it yourself.

> **Come With Me**
> *You don't see the scope of this battle, but I do.*

Jesus led his followers into a culture of consideration over condemnation. When we exchange consideration for condemnation, we consider what a person might be walking through before responding. When we exchange consideration for condemnation, we consider the burden another bears.

Long before we accuse or point a finger, we bring it to prayer.

There just might be something God wants to show us.

Father, our hearts naturally jump to judgment. Reveal what we cannot see in the natural. Change the conversation as you enter in.

PUSH OUT DEEPER: Luke 6:37–38; James 2:13; James 3:17; Matthew 18:31–33

Pressed Down, Shaken Together

"Give, and you will receive. Your gift will return to you in full—
pressed down, shaken together to make room for more, running
over, and poured into your lap. The amount you give will determine
the amount you get back."

LUKE 6:38 NLT

EN WEAR DRAPED ROBES bound with a girdle with a generous fold over the chest. A merchant pours grain or other goods directly into the lap or "bosom" of that garment. Grain is pressed down and shaken together to make room for more. While this passage seems to be about money, Jesus is not speaking about money at all. He's describing a different currency—withholding criticism and offering generous forgiveness.

> **Come With Me**
> *What you don't say
> can be as generous as
> what you do say.*

The measure of kindness or criticism we offer determines the portion we receive. We are accountable for our words. They nestle into the heart of a child, a friend, a spouse, or that stranger. May our words and actions be kindhearted and sincere.

Overflowing.

Shaken together.

Running over as we pour into the lives of others.

PUSH OUT DEEPER: Luke 6:38; Proverbs 11:25; 2 Corinthians 9:6; Galatians 6:9

Like the Teacher

"A student is no better than his teacher. But everyone who is well-trained will be like his teacher."

LUKE 6:40 GW

THE DISCIPLES CRASH into uncertainty numerous times. They are the students and Jesus is the teacher.

What do we do now?

Where do we go?

Lord, are you sure you are asking us to do this?

Finding answers through feelings is akin to the blind leading the blind. Feelings pop up out of nowhere. Opinion is plentiful. Doubt causes us to stumble.

When we turn to Jesus, it's a safe place.

The fact that we are uncertain doesn't mean our heavenly Father doesn't know exactly where we are going.

If we are open to learning, he's consistently teaching.

> **Come With Me**
>
> *There are no wrong questions, and I have the right answers for you.*

There's no shame in asking questions, as long as we go to him for the answers.

PUSH OUT DEEPER: Luke 6:39–41; John 15:1; Matthew 11:29; 1 Peter 2:21

I'm Still Here

"He is like a person who dug down to bedrock to lay the foundation of his home. When a flood came, the floodwaters pushed against that house. But the house couldn't be washed away because it had a good foundation."

LUKE 6:48 GW

A STORM IS DANGEROUS to the house built on sand. Wind stirs in the mountains, creating tumultuous squalls along the seashore. Sand shifts and blows away, and the house tumbles down.

Not so for the house built upon the rock.

Why would anyone build a house on sand? Because it's easier. The rock Jesus describes in this parable is native rock that rises up through the earth. It's sturdy and unmovable, so a person has to excavate deep to find it. It takes longer, but the builder who secures his home with such solid groundwork has a greater chance of standing strong in a storm.

Oh, the lessons in this story!

Life will batter us. Squalls blow out of nowhere. Trials come.

When we safeguard our heart in the Rock of Ages, we are anchored. It's easier to settle for shallow faith, but when we tie ourselves to unmovable faith, the calm in our hearts is far greater.

> ### Come With Me
> Anchor your soul in what cannot be stolen, swept away, or destroyed.

PUSH OUT DEEPER: Luke 6:47–49; Isaiah 28:16; Nahum 1:7; Proverbs 10:25

Delight

When Jesus heard this, he was amazed at him, and turning to the
crowd following him, he said, "I tell you, I have not found such
great faith even in Israel."

LUKE 7:9 NIV

A CENTURION OWNS a slave who is deathly ill. He sends Jewish leaders to ask Jesus to come quickly. On the way to the
centurion's quarters, Jesus receives a second message. The centurion
tells Jesus he's not worthy of Jesus coming to his home. He asks Jesus to
pray right where he is, believing that is enough
to heal his servant.

Jesus commends his faith.

This centurion is known for his good deeds.
His actions reveal kindheartedness. All of these
things are good qualities, yet it is his faith that
delights Jesus.

> **Come With Me**
> *Your good heart is
> a beautiful thing,
> but your faith in
> me is inspiring.*

Our good works are noticed. They make a dif-
ference in our communities. Kindness changes our relationships. These
outward characteristics are pleasing.

When we combine good works with faith in God, it delights the
heart of our Lord. Perhaps people notice, or maybe they don't. God
sees it every time.

PUSH OUT DEEPER: Luke 7:1–10; Job 42:5; Galatians 3:2; Romans 1:16

Arise

He went up to the open coffin, took hold of it, and the men who were carrying it stopped. He said, "Young man, I'm telling you to come back to life!"

LUKE 7:14 GW

THE BEREAVED MOM trudges behind the coffin. She has already lost her husband. Losing her son is tragic. It leaves her alone and unprotected.

Jesus and his band of followers pass by. Jesus slows when he sees the procession. He puts his hands on the bier and speaks to the boy as if he is already alive.

One breath, and then another!

Jesus gives the woman back her son, but also her life.

There are many forms of death. It can steal our dreams. A marriage can be on the brink. Whatever death is trying to steal, our Savior notices.

He stops. He places his hands over our dying hopes. He breathes on the burning embers of our God-given hopes.

> ### Come With Me
> *If I am the author of a dream or desire, I can bring new life to it.*

Jesus, when it seems that death has robbed us, we acknowledge that you are life. Thank you for seeing what we are going through and stopping to linger. Thank you for placing your hands on the embers and bringing them back to life.

PUSH OUT DEEPER: Luke 7:11–17; Acts 26:8; John 5:21; John 6:63

Revolutionary Faith

And he answered them, "Go and tell John what you have seen and heard: the blind receive their sight, the lame walk, lepers are cleansed, and the deaf hear, the dead are raised up, the poor have good news preached to them."

LUKE 7:22 ESV

JOHN THE BAPTIST is still in prison, and he sends his followers to ask Jesus a question. *Are you the Messiah?*

John believes in Jesus. He always has. His question reveals his troubled feelings. He thought Jesus would come as a king. Jesus sends a message back to John through his disciples. *Tell them what you've seen.*

They tell John that Jesus prayed and they were made whole. They tell him about the lepers, the forsaken, and how he battles the hypocritical religious establishment. They tell John that Jesus preaches a gospel of hope.

Jesus didn't come as an earthly king. He never tried to overthrow governments. He never claimed earthly authority.

Jesus came to bring men and women into right relationship with God.

> **Come With Me**
> *My greatest work in and through you is a result of mercy.*

Faith is not force. It's not grand plans or grand organizations. Without the love of God, those institutions fail.

Faith that changes the world is revolutionary faith, showing mercy in the trenches.

PUSH OUT DEEPER: Luke 7:18–22; Isaiah 42:1–4; Philippians 2:6–7; Mark 10:45

Different

> And he added, "God blesses those who do not fall away because of me."
>
> LUKE 7:23 NLT

JESUS ASKS JOHN to hold on a little longer. When John the Baptist shouted to the crowds that a Messiah was coming, it was true. When John baptized Jesus and heard a voice from heaven, the words were from God himself.

Jesus is exactly who John believes him to be—the Savior of the world. His reign on earth might not look like John thought it would, but that doesn't negate Jesus' identity. God had a plan from the beginning, and both Jesus and John were a part of it.

We can feel low when God plants a dream and it's harder than we thought. We may wonder if God is anywhere in sight. It is taking longer than we thought it should.

Come With Me

It might not look like your plan, but I have one. Trusting me is part of that plan.

Faith is moving forward, trusting that we heard the voice of God speak.

One step. One prayer. One small act of faith. Each is part of the journey. No part is wasted. It doesn't have to be our way, our plan, or our timing for his eternal impact to unfold.

PUSH OUT DEEPER: Luke 7:22–23; Psalm 33:11; Proverbs 19:21; Isaiah 55:8

45

Least of These

"I tell you, among those born of women there is no one greater than John; yet the one who is least in the kingdom of God is greater than he."

LUKE 7:28 NIV

JESUS LISTENS to the small child who feels invisible. He touches the leper. Women are seen as worthy. There are no castes, no divides, no person more deserving due to wealth or position or any other factor in the eyes of Jesus.

The least in Jesus' kingdom is among the greatest.

Jesus wove a message of equality through his teaching, but more so by his example. In our uneven world it's easy to overlook a child who hides quietly in the background. We may see the behavior, but not the home life. It might be tempting to look past that refugee clutching her child to her chest. What about that recovering addict whose backstory is far from pretty?

> **Come With Me**
> *There is no person underserving of my love.*

Jesus sees them, but will we?

Often the greatest gift we can give is to notice someone.

See that one who is unsure if God cares for him.

Let's show that one God's love as we pay attention. One person can't address the needs of the entire world, but when we all begin to notice, our culture shifts. God loves the least of these, and when we love them, that becomes their truth.

PUSH OUT DEEPER: Luke 7:28; 1 Corinthians 1:27; James 2:5; 1 Samuel 2:8

Set Apart

But the Pharisees and the experts in Moses' Teachings rejected
God's plan for them. They refused to be baptized.

LUKE 7:30 GW

BAPTISM IS MORE than a dunk in a muddy river. It is a public
proclamation. It signifies rebirth from sin to righteousness and
immediately sets a person apart.

The Pharisees and experts refuse to be baptized. By doing so, they
send a clear message. When they reject baptism, they reject God's plan
for them.

Baptism still distinguishes believers in all parts of the world. In
many countries, a public act of faith such as baptism marks a person
for persecution.

> ### Come With Me
> *Tell everyone you know
> that you are mine.*

They step into the water knowing that family
might turn away.

They choose baptism even if it might result in
imprisonment or death.

When they choose baptism, they choose Jesus.

Baptism is more than ritual. It's not how we do it. It's that we can't wait
to tell everyone we know that we are his—not because of our goodness,
but because of the cross.

PUSH OUT DEEPER: Luke 7:29–30; Acts 13:24; Acts 19:4; 2 Corinthians 4:8–10

47

Alabaster Tears

Now when the Pharisee who had invited Him saw this, he spoke
to himself, saying, "This Man, if He were a prophet, would know
who and what manner of woman this is who is touching Him,
for she is a sinner."

LUKE 7:39 NKJV

A SINFUL WOMAN kneels at the feet of Jesus and tears drip on
his feet. She dries them with her hair, kissing his feet over and
over again. The astonished host looks on as she breaks a flask of expensive
perfume and pours it over Jesus' feet like an offering.

Simon, a Pharisee, is shocked that Jesus doesn't know who is touching him.

We may be tempted to judge Simon, because
he lacks compassion. Before we judge, let's first
hold up a mirror and study ourselves.

When we meet that one whose sin is great, do
we judge her silently? When we meet that one
desperate for forgiveness, do we offer condemnation instead?

> ### Come With Me
> *Do you remember
> when you first came
> to me? Share with me
> what you remember
> about that day.*

The woman who knelt at Jesus' feet was a sinner, but so was Simon. We have all sinned. Let's remember back to the
time we first knelt at Jesus' feet. Let's praise him for how far he's taken us
since that day. When tempted to choose between mercy and judgment,
let's offer the gift we received for ourselves.

PUSH OUT DEEPER: Luke 7:36–39; Ecclesiastes 7:20; Acts 26:18; 1 John 2:12

Who Loves Him More?

"A certain moneylender had two debtors. One owed five hundred denarii, and the other fifty. When they could not pay, he cancelled the debt of both. Now which of them will love him more?"

LUKE 7:41–42 ESV

WE DON'T KNOW how the sinful woman knew Jesus. She may have stood on the fringes to hear him speak. She may have heard him say he came to mend the wounded. Perhaps her heart leaped at the thought that God had not abandoned her due to her sin.

Certainly, she trembled at the scrutiny of the crowd. She was unliked. Unwanted.

She dared to walk into the room because Jesus was there.

Only Jesus could clear her debt.

> **Come With Me**
> *Your slate is clear. I have paid the price. Don't hold on to the past anymore.*

Our sin is too great for us to remove on our own, but not for Jesus. We can always come to him, no matter who believes otherwise. Jesus takes our sin and writes in his own blood, "Paid in full."

Who loves Jesus more?

Every one of us whose debt rests upon him, our peace upon his brow.

PUSH OUT DEEPER: Luke 7:40–43; Romans 5:19; Hebrews 12:2; 1 Peter 2:24

He's With Us

Then he turned to the woman and said to Simon, "Look at this woman kneeling here. When I entered your home, you didn't offer me water to wash the dust from my feet, but she has washed them with her tears and wiped them with her hair."

LUKE 7:44 NLT

WHEN ANY GUEST WALKS through the door, a servant quickly washes the guest's dusty feet. When it is an honored guest, the person is met by the host. He kisses the honored guest's cheek, anoints his head with oil, and gently washes his feet until they are clean.

Simon did none of those things.

This break in hospitality is more than an oversight. It reveals Simon's attitude toward Jesus.

Jesus is in our midst. Do we take his presence for granted?

He's as close as a whisper. Do we value that intimacy?

He counsels us when we don't know what to do.

> ### Come With Me
> *I'm more than a habit. I'm the Creator of the universe. I'm omniscient, and sovereign. I'm also your friend.*

He is friend. He is Lord. Are we callous to the magnitude of these gifts?

Let's kiss his cheek in gratitude. Let's anoint his head with oil as we seek his presence. Let's wash his feet as we say thank-you.

Thank you, Lord, for your presence. We can't imagine life without you. We are humbled by your love. We notice your many gifts, and the greatest of these is you.

PUSH OUT DEEPER: Luke 7:43–46; Psalm 51:10–12; 1 Peter 1:25; Psalm 114:7

In His Eyes

"But whoever receives little forgiveness loves very little."

LUKE 7:47 GW

E YES FOLLOW the sinful woman.

One looks at her with sorrow, for the fallen woman is responsible for the damage in her marriage.

Some follow in fear that she will tell their secrets.

Others follow with lust.

Jesus' eyes are different. He sees the possibilities of who she can become. Her sin has hurt others. Her sins have caused her parents to hang their heads in embarrassment. Her sin has produced tears for those whose marriages she has wrecked.

Yet in Jesus' eyes there is hope for change.

No matter the depth of our transgressions, there is always hope. It may seem impossible, but Jesus cracks open hardened hearts. No sin is greater than another or beyond his reach.

> ## Come With Me
> I have come to release the power of sin over your life.

In an astonishing act of graciousness, he released us from the bonds of every offense. When we come to him in repentance, he forgives.

He has forgiven much, and we cannot help but love him in return.

PUSH OUT DEEPER: Luke 7:47–49; Matthew 20:33–34; Isaiah 35:5; Romans 6:22

Loosed!

After this, Jesus traveled about from one town and village to another, proclaiming the good news of the kingdom of God. The
Twelve were with him, and also some women who had been cured
of evil spirits and diseases: Mary (called Magdalene) from whom
seven demons had come out. . . .

LUKE 8:1–2 NIV

WHEN JESUS CAST the seven demons from Mary Magdalene,
her anguish ended. Her life was so dramatically altered that
she believed in Jesus from that day forward. She became a friend to Jesus
because he was a friend to her. He crushed evil on her behalf.

We might struggle with the thought of demonic influence in a
modern-day world, but we cannot deny that evil
exists. Jesus' healing power brought *shalom*—
flourishing wholeness—to Mary Magdalene. That
same power thrives today.

Our prayers march into shadowy places where
wickedness exists and shake the foundation of evil.

Because of Jesus, the irreparably broken and
damaged is pieced back together beautifully. Evil exists, but Jesus is
greater.

The power of evil is shattered in Jesus' name.

> ### Come With Me
> *Don't counter evil
> in your own power,
> but march toward
> it in mine.*

PUSH OUT DEEPER: Luke 8:1–3; Mark 16:9; Luke 10:19; Romans 16:20

Parable of Thorns

"And some fell among thorns, and the thorns grew up with it and choked it."

LUKE 8:7 ESV

THE SOWER CARRIES a bag of seed to a distant, uncultivated plot of land. This land consists of some fertile ground, some shallow and hard-packed, and some that is wild with weeds and thorns.

In the thorny region, thistle plants grow as high as a man's head. Seeds have little chance of sprouting without a covering of rich soil. They are brutally exposed to the sun, and seeds wither and blow away.

These thorns represent our cares and riches of the world. Cares trap us in the thistles of worry. On the other hand, riches distract us as we while away our time and energy on things that will eventually disintegrate.

> ### Come With Me
> Don't plant your life in thorny ground, but in fertile soil. Watch the blessings grow.

When we cast our cares upon him, we sow seed in fertile ground. His broad shoulders are wide enough to carry our burdens. When we sow our riches in the kingdom, it becomes a means of blessing, rather than a distraction.

Our time on earth is short. The growing season is brief.

Let us plant our worries and our riches where they will produce the greatest harvest.

PUSH OUT DEEPER: Luke 8:6–9; Ezekiel 7:8; Psalm 92:12; Psalm 1:3

Roots

"Still other seed fell on good soil. It came up and yielded a crop, a hundred times more than was sown." When he said this, he called out, "Whoever has ears to hear, let them hear."

LUKE 8:8 NIV

T HE DISCIPLES don't always understand what Jesus teaches. In fact, some of his teaching won't make sense until after the cross. Every crop takes time to mature, and the disciples are no different.

We are also a work in progress.

Spiritual maturity isn't a footrace, but a lifetime of walking with Jesus.

As we read his Word and gather with other believers, seeds are planted. As our beliefs are put to the test, sprouts form. As we live out our faith, roots push down and take hold. Then comes a sweet season as we bear fruit.

> ### Come With Me
> *Take your eyes off others and let me show you what I have for you.*

We won't always have all the answers. There will be times that it seems a friend's growth process is ten times more productive than our own. Our faith in Christ is not a contest. Every part of our walk with Jesus matters, not just to us but to God.

He plants, he waters, and the harvest springs forth in each of us.

Our part is simply to be good soil, open and receptive to all that he desires to teach.

PUSH OUT DEEPER: Luke 8:8–9; John 12:16; John 20:9; James 1:4

54

Parables

And He said, "To you it has been given to know the mysteries of the kingdom of God, but to the rest it is given in parables, that 'Seeing they may not see, and hearing they may not understand.'"

THE DISCIPLES don't need parables, for they have Jesus right next to them. The Word of God is with them every day. Jesus won't always be with the disciples, at least not in the flesh, but he promises to send another teacher.

They will have one who will take Jesus' words and bring them to life. When the Word of God feels like a mystery, we can pray for the Holy Spirit to teach us. He removes the veil from the Word so that we might see it.

In seeing, we hear. In hearing, we understand. When we understand, we begin to live it.

We take heart that our faith isn't a mystery, but a discovery process. Layer by layer, his Word is made manifest. If we come to faith later in life, the Holy Spirit expedites our learning. If we have not always consumed his Word, our hunger for it grows as we step into the pages.

His Word reaches for us. It teaches us.

The Holy Spirit removes the barriers from our understanding as it changes us.

> ### Come With Me
>
> *When you don't understand, ask me. I'll open the eyes of your spirit.*

PUSH OUT DEEPER: Luke 8:10–15; 1 Thessalonians 2:13; Hebrews 4:12; Jeremiah 23:29

We Are the Light

> "No one lights a lamp and hides it under a bowl or puts it under a bed. Instead, everyone who lights a lamp puts it on a lamp stand so that those who come in will see the light."
>
> LUKE 8:16 GW

WHEN JESUS CHOSE THE TWELVE, he started a movement. One light kindled the flame of another. A church was planted. A disciple made. A baptism performed.

The Word was taught. Prayer sparked fire and faith spread.

These ordinary followers became light.

All together, they burned brightly. The gospel blazed from city to city and from generation to generation.

> ### Come With Me
> *When my church puts their lights together, the brightness cannot be extinguished.*

Today it still burns. We are that light. We cannot hide it, for it's a torch passed down, all the way from Jesus. That light has the power to rescue those trapped in darkness. It may flicker. It may blaze. When we bring our lights together, it reaches to dispel the shadows.

Savior, we are your disciples. May we put our lamps together to shine a light on you. Unite us as your followers. Burn brightly in your church one more time.

PUSH OUT DEEPER: Luke 8:16–17; 2 Corinthians 4:6; Acts 26:18; Acts 7:58

Listen

"So pay attention to how you hear. To those who listen to my teaching, more understanding will be given. But for those who are not listening, even what they think they understand will be taken away from them."

LUKE 8:18 NLT

THERE ARE ALL KINDS of hearers. Some receive what Jesus says. Others reject it. Some are good soil. Some are not. Regardless of the response, there is no ground that is hopeless.

Thorns can be yanked up from the root. Rocks can be discharged through the power of prayer. Fallow ground can be tilled and nurtured until it is ready for harvest.

> **Come With Me**
> *You've planted that seed in faith. I'll water it. I'll watch over it. One day we'll celebrate a harvest.*

As followers of Christ, we will meet thorny people. As believers, we will plant seed in rocky ground.

We can become discouraged when we don't see the harvest. It's not our efforts that produce a crop, however. It's planting when and where he instructs. As seed sowers, we are not swayed by rocky soil, fallow ground, or thorns.

We sow our portion of seeds and trust his timing. We remember his promises, even when we don't see a right-now result.

We wait for life to push through the soil.

We let it grow in God's timing, as he brings the harvest to completion.

PUSH OUT DEEPER: Luke 8:17–18; Isaiah 58:11; John 7:38; John 6:51

More to Do

Someone told him, "Your mother and brothers are standing outside, wanting to see you."

LUKE 8:20 NIV

MARY TRAVELS to see her son, Jesus. She is worried about him. She senses that Jesus is tired, and indeed he is. He's been teaching for days and ministering to the sick.

Jesus loves his mother deeply, and he isn't disrespectful. His time on earth isn't long. He refuses to allow her worries to stop him from doing his Father's work.

Our faith may lead in a direction that makes others anxious.

Perhaps God's plan isn't their plan for us, so they worry. Perhaps they would choose a safer life or an easier path for us, if we'd just listen.

Isn't it beautiful when the people we love care about us?

> ### Come With Me
> *When others struggle to understand the path I've placed you on, I understand. Bring those concerns to me.*

We are wise to listen to those who have our best interests at heart, yet God is the greater authority.

Jesus, help us to unpack the advice of those who love us. Remind us to be thankful there are people who care about us. If there's wisdom to be found in their words, open our ears to hear. If their worries do not reflect your heart, let us stay the course. Soothe their troubled hearts as we choose your will.

PUSH OUT DEEPER: Luke 8:19–21; 1 Peter 3:15; Proverbs 15:1; Proverbs 25:15

Be Still

As they were sailing along, Jesus fell asleep. A violent storm came across the lake. The boat was taking on water, and they were in danger.

LUKE 8:23 GW

A DARK CLOUD FORMS quickly over the boat. It rocks on wave-capped waters as Jesus sleeps, blissfully unaware. Some try to bail the water from the boat, but to no avail. Others cling to the sides of the boat, shouting the Messiah's name until he awakens.

Jesus points at the dark clouds and demands they be still. His words are just as much for the soaking wet men as for the heavens.

Hadn't he assured them they would reach the other side?

Be still.

These words are spoken over us when storms sweep in.

We aren't guaranteed a storm-free life, but we are assured that he's in the storm with us. Our faith is not shipwrecked. The storm will pass and the clouds will clear.

While the storm rages, his power is not at rest. It holds us in the boat and establishes our faith. It quiets our pounding hearts and calms our fears.

> ## Come With Me
> *Be still, my child, as we pass through the storm together.*

PUSH OUT DEEPER: Luke 8:22–24; Zechariah 10:11; Isaiah 51:10; Psalm 46:10

Shipwrecked

"Where is your faith?" he asked his disciples. In fear and amazement they asked one another, "Who is this? He commands even the winds and the water, and they obey him."

LUKE 8:25 NIV

THE DISCIPLES COLLAPSE in relief as the boat glides toward the shore. The water is like silk, and the skies have settled. Jesus sits next to them.

Where was your faith, guys?

The truth is that they were worried about Jesus. He was asleep in the boat and could have easily been tossed over the side. They all could have perished! Stakes were higher than a tempest or falling overboard. If the boat capsized and they all drowned, who would continue the work of the kingdom?

> **Come With Me**
> *Hold fast to me in a storm. Don't let go. Be still and know that I'm God.*

When we are in a storm, our first thoughts might not be of our own well-being. We worry over a marriage, a child, a ministry, a work of the heart.

We pray that this good work won't be shipwrecked.

No one wants to go through a storm, especially in a ministry, a marriage, a child, or a work of the heart. Just as Jesus promised they'd reach the other side, we hold on until we reach the shore.

A storm cannot demolish his promises. Let's trust him with our most precious gifts as he takes us to the other side.

PUSH OUT DEEPER: Luke 8:24–25; Psalm 107:2; Psalm 55:8; Isaiah 25:4

Unshackled

The people went to see what had happened. They came to Jesus and found the man from whom the demons had gone out. Dressed and in his right mind, he was sitting at Jesus' feet. The people were frightened.

LUKE 8:35 GW

THE DEMONIAC LIVES IN A CEMETERY, homeless and naked. When the boat pushes onto shore, he rushes to meet Jesus. He shrieks and falls down in front of him.

Jesus tames the unruly legion of dark spirits residing in this man, and sends them into a herd of pigs. Two thousand swine rush over the side of the mountain and plunge to their deaths.

> ### Come With Me
> *When tempted to mourn what once held you hostage, remember the freedom that now lives inside of you.*

The crowd is angry. Though a man once shackled by demons is completely whole, they are oblivious. The crowd is less impressed by the man clothed and in his right mind than by the forbidden pork they nurtured on the hillside.

Jesus releases our handcuffs of sin, and we leave behind things we once nurtured—like resentment, insecurity, or self-defeating behaviors. Sin plunges to death, and new life springs forth.

The enemy will tempt us to look back at what we lost or to nurture those things that are forbidden. That's when we remind him we've been loosed!

We have no cause to look back, but to rejoice in what we've gained.

PUSH OUT DEEPER: Luke 8:26–37; Proverbs 26:11; Romans 6:1; 1 Timothy 1:13–14

Tell Everyone

"Return to your home, and declare how much God has done for you." And he went away, proclaiming throughout the whole city how much Jesus had done for him.

LUKE 8:39 ESV

THE MAN ONCE TRAPPED AND TORTURED by demons asks to follow Jesus.

Who can blame him?

Just that morning he was bound, but now he's free. Jesus asks him to stay in his own community. Why? It's where his influence will be the greatest. This man's healing will astound relatives who didn't know how to fix him. His story will surprise strong men sent to chain him up when his behavior was out of control.

Though he won't follow Jesus physically, his story will lead others to Jesus.

When asked to share our story, we might struggle with the request. It's easier to share it with those who don't know our history. We wonder if people will mistrust our faith or wait for us to mess up. They might even remind us of the days when we were bound in sin.

Come With Me
Write it down. Share it with others. Let me use your story for my good.

It might take time for them to believe, and that's okay. His work is genuine. Our healing reflects his glory. If one is not ready to hear, there's another desperate to listen.

Jesus healed us and he'll give us the courage to share our stories.

PUSH OUT DEEPER: Luke 8:38–39; Deuteronomy 10:21; Psalm 145:6; Jeremiah 17:14

Reach for His Hem

The woman saw that she couldn't hide. Trembling, she quickly bowed in front of him. There, in front of all the people, she told why she touched him and how she was cured at once.

LUKE 8:47 GW

FOR TWELVE YEARS her condition has left her anemic and fatigued. She's been to every doctor in town, but they've given up on her. One day, as Jesus and the disciples walk down the street in a crushing mob, she takes a risk.

She reaches for the hem of his garment, hoping he won't know she's touched him. When Jesus stops, she confesses.

It's me. I'm the one who touched the hem of your garment.

Instead of condemnation, she receives a cleansing. Her entire life is transformed. She is no longer bleeding. She is no longer isolated. What the doctors couldn't do, a single touch of the hem of his garment did.

> **Come With Me**
> *Touch the hem of my garment. Touch my hands.*

When we need Jesus, we don't have to hide in shame. Our unclean state—no matter what it is—is not the deciding factor in God's mercy.

He feels our tentative touch, and it's more than enough.

Jesus, we reach for the hem of your garment in faith.

PUSH OUT DEEPER: Luke 8:43–48; Leviticus 15:25; Matthew 8:17; Matthew 14:35–36

I Was First

But the crowd laughed at him because they all knew she had died.

LUKE 8:53 NLT

JAIRUS PACES RESTLESSLY as Jesus takes precious time with the woman with the issue of blood. His twelve-year-old girl is at home dying. He had bowed before Jesus. That's uncommon for any ruler, but he's a desperate daddy.

More minutes pass. Time is of the essence. If only Jesus will hurry.

Finally, the woman is healed and they leave. When they arrive, the mourners are already singing their sorrowful song.

It's too late.

Jesus pushes past the mourners. Moments later, Jairus's daughter dashes into her daddy's arms.

It's challenging when we were first and feel that we are last.

> **Come With Me**
> *I heard you. I'm working on your miracle in ways you cannot see.*

We asked God for help, but others prosper in front of us. We waited our turn, and we are still waiting. We are plied with advice from cynics, even if it's our own critical voice.

His power is not like sand in an hourglass, running out as others receive their answers. He hears every prayer. He sees every child of God. He hears our prayers the moment we speak them.

Jesus, help us to be patient as you perform that miracle on our behalf.

PUSH OUT DEEPER: Luke 8:41–42; Luke 8:49–56; 1 Corinthians 2:5; 2 Corinthians 12:9

Dynamis!

Jesus called the twelve apostles together and gave them power and authority over every demon and power and authority to cure diseases.

LUKE 9:1 GW

PRINCIPALITIES AND PRINCES of the air shake at the name of Jesus. They tremble as the disciples confront them, though they aren't the best speakers in town. They don't have the most money. Their feet are caked in dirt from traveling, and their cloaks are dusty.

Instead, they are anointed.

When he says go, he does not leave us ill-equipped.

We are anointed with *dynamis* power.

Our confidence is not found in substitutes like charisma or charm. It's not our great marketing plan or how talented we are. It's not our eloquence or how measureless our resources.

Without his power, we are ill-equipped, so we place our confidence in him long before we place it in things or people. This anointing only comes through the Holy Spirit. We find it as we seek the presence of God.

When we *go* in that authority, darkness quakes at the body of Christ.

> ## Come With Me
> I have anointed you, and you have what you need.

PUSH OUT DEEPER: Luke 9:1–2; Romans 15:13; Romans 15:19; 2 Corinthians 12:12

For the Road

"Take nothing for your journey," he instructed them. "Don't take a walking stick, a traveler's bag, food, money, or even a change of clothes."

LUKE 9:3 NLT

A S JESUS AND THE DISCIPLES enter a city, they immediately seek a mission house. In that home, they are greeted with open arms. They are fed and given a bed. A mission home provides refuge after a long day of wearying ministry. Neighbors and family members dine with them in the evening. Thus, they are further bolstered as they share community.

A mission house is a haven for these weary road warriors.

Fatigued warriors live among us.

Missionaries, pastors, teachers, ministry leaders, and workers sacrifice comforts in order to do the work of Jesus.

They too need a safe place to land.

Let us be a refuge for one another. Ease others' loads by providing a safe place with our words. Lighten their burdens with genuine hospitality and a kind word. When we minister to weary warriors, we minister to the One for which they labor.

> **Come With Me**
> *Words of criticism tear down my hardest workers, but your encouragement creates a safe environment.*

PUSH OUT DEEPER: Luke 9:2–4; Philemon 1:17; 2 Corinthians 8:23; Philippians 2:25

Travel Light

> "If people do not welcome you, leave their town and shake the
> dust off your feet as a testimony against them."
>
> LUKE 9:5 NIV

WHEN THE JEWISH PEOPLE left exile generations earlier, they shook the dust from their feet. In part, it was a statement against the abuse they left behind. It also symbolized a new beginning. They didn't have time for revenge. They had places to go and a promised land to conquer.

The disciples are instructed to travel light. They carry no earthly possessions. No baggage. Their resources are inner strength and the direction of the Holy Spirit. If they land in a city where their message is unwelcome, they shake the dust from their feet.

Still they travel light. Though they are treated unwell, they aren't weighed down. They keep going. There are people to pray for and a message to share.

Come With Me
Show the message with your life if they don't understand the words.

We live in a culture where faith is often misinterpreted. The response may be antagonistic. We travel light as we shake the dust from our hearts. We travel light as we shake it from our attitudes. We don't know why they believe the way they do, but our role is to share the message. If they aren't ready, we pray for them and continue to love them, but we keep going—our burden light.

PUSH OUT DEEPER: Luke 9:2–4; Luke 21:19; Romans 2:7; Psalm 121:8

Tell Jesus

On their return the apostles told him all that they had done. And
he took them and withdrew apart to a town called Bethsaida.

LUKE 9:10 ESV

THEY ARE LIKE LITTLE CHILDREN running from the bus after the
first day of school. The newly appointed disciples can't wait to tell
Jesus everything. They had accepted their assignment with apprehension, but by the end of the day, there were converts. Miracles took place.
Even demons fled in Jesus' name!

Imagine what it would be like to share our faith adventures with Jesus.

A marriage was in trouble, but love is in the air.

A friend read the Bible for the first time, and it opened her eyes to
truth.

A child was having difficulty at school, but
after prayer it eased.

Talking with Jesus is more than asking for
what we need.

It's a personal conversation between us and
God. We celebrate as we reflect on answered prayer. We stop to savor
a sunrise. We talk with him all day. What an honor it is to run to him,
celebrating all the good things he has done.

> ### Come With Me
> *I love to hear about the good things in your life.*

PUSH OUT DEEPER: Luke 9:10–11; 1 Corinthians 1:9; 1 John 1:3; Matthew 6:2–4

You Feed Them

> He replied, "You give them something to eat." They answered, "We have only five loaves of bread and two fish—unless we go and buy food for all this crowd."
>
> LUKE 9:13 NIV

JESUS AND HIS FRIENDS withdraw to a remote area of Bethsaida. Five thousand men with their wives and children follow. After Jesus teaches all day, the disciples worry about how to feed the crowd. There isn't enough money in the treasury, so a few of the disciples try to convince Jesus to send them away. It's a hike, but they can travel to a nearby town and eat and rest.

Jesus issues a startling request. *You feed them.*

The disciples stare out over the multitude. All they have is a few fish and loaves of bread. It isn't enough to feed themselves, much less a multitude.

Jesus wasn't asking them to provide the miracle, but to give him what they had.

When Jesus asks us to believe in something big, he's not asking us to perform the miracle. We are not responsible to make it happen. He's asking us to bring what we do have to him. Every bit of it. We aren't in this by ourselves.

When we give him all we have, even when it seems small, that act of obedience just might be the beginning of our greatest miracle.

> ### Come With Me
> *Give me your doubts. Give me your hopes. Give me your talent. Give me your life. I'll be in charge of the miracles.*

PUSH OUT DEEPER: Luke 9:11–17; Mark 4:31–32; 1 Kings 17:11–16; Mark 12:43–44

69

Leftovers

And they all ate and were satisfied. And what was left over was picked up, twelve baskets of broken pieces.

LUKE 9:17 ESV

THE LEFTOVERS fill twelve rope baskets!

Each basket is a reminder of the abundant provision received. The disciples don't leave any extra in the hot sun to ruin. They treat the extra as heavenly provision. It will feed the poor and the widows in the next leg of their journey.

There are seasons when we don't have enough, but also seasons when we have more than enough. What will we do with that abundant provision? Rather than squander it or leave it in storehouses to gather dust, we can use it in the next leg of ministry.

Perhaps we bless a start-up with big dreams. Perhaps we pay a light bill for a single mom. Perhaps we pay for a meal or secretly make a Christmas bright for a child.

> **Come With Me**
>
> *Some of the greatest treasures you will ever accumulate will be the ones you gave away.*

God will show us what to do with the goodness of his gift. Our overflowing basket becomes an answer to prayer for someone in the *not enough* season of their life.

Thank you, Lord, for this season of more than enough. Show us one way to be a blessing to someone who is struggling. Thank you for allowing us to be a part of answered prayer.

PUSH OUT DEEPER: Luke 9:16–17; Luke 12:33; Matthew 6:19; Acts 2:45

Jesus, the Christ

One day Jesus left the crowds to pray alone. Only his disciples
were with him, and he asked them, "Who do people say I am?"

LUKE 9:18 NLT

ONCE UPON A TIME Herod the King asked about the identity of
Jesus. It was after he ordered the beheading of John the Baptist.
When he heard about the feats of Jesus, he feared John had come back
to life in the form of the teacher.

Now Jesus asks the disciples the same question. *Who do you think
I am?*

Peter answers quickly. *You are Jesus, the Christ.*

Not just Jesus, my friend, or Jesus, the teacher, but Jesus, the Christ.
Jesus is Lord.

We hear about Jesus in sermons. We are taught what faith looks
like. Personal faith is birthed as we experience
him for ourselves.

Certainly he's a friend. A comfort. A source
of strength. We discover these and other good
traits about Jesus. Then there's the most powerful
truth of all.

Jesus is the Christ. He's Lord! He's worthy of
worship. He's worthy of obedience. He's worthy of loyalty. As we believe
this personally, our faith becomes more than hearsay.

Come With Me
*Who do you say I
am? I am your Lord,
Jesus the Christ.*

PUSH OUT DEEPER: Luke 9:18–20; Luke 9:7–9; Romans 10:9; 1 John 4:15

Self-Emptied

> And he said to them all, If any man will come after me, let him
> deny himself, and take up his cross daily, and follow me.
>
> LUKE 9:23 KJV

WHEN JESUS IMPLIES that following him equals carrying a cross, he reveals a life-changing principle.

When we carry our cross daily, we live self-emptied.

We place less importance on what *we* want in order to discover what *he* wants. We trust his leading over plowing our own path. We give his instructions greater weight than how we feel. Living self-emptied powerfully changes how we spend our time and the way we love others. It labels those things that have little value, or allows us to release those things that have far too much influence over our hearts.

When we live self-emptied, it makes more room for Jesus.

> **Come With Me**
>
> *Denying yourself allows you to discover your God-filled self.*

That's an incredible exchange! We are self-emptied, but full of the Holy Spirit. We are self-emptied, but filled with direction. We are self-emptied, but overflowing with His presence. When we carry our cross, we deny ourselves, releasing those things that crowd out our faith. In doing so, we discover who we are.

PUSH OUT DEEPER: Luke 9:23–25; 2 Corinthians 13:5; John 19:17; Ephesians 3:17–19

Like Jesus

For whosoever will save his life shall lose it: but whosoever will
lose his life for my sake, the same shall save it.

LUKE 9:24 KJV

IT IS HUMAN TO WORRY about our lives, take care of our feelings,
and manage our own agenda. The disciples' thoughts, however, slowly
transition from their own lives to death. Not death in the natural, but
death to things that don't really help them live at all.

They are starting to live like Jesus. Generosity is birthed as selfish-
ness is denied. Compassion is kindled when unkindness is refused. The
more they say no, the greater room to say yes to all the plans Jesus has
for them. In the end, most of the disciples will be martyred for their
faith and profess Jesus to the end—because of
their relationship with Christ, their lives were full!

When we get to the end of our lives, what
will define us?

It will be the things we hang on to.

We have a choice in what we hold close and
what we hold loosely. We can hang on to resent-
ment, unforgiveness, comparison, or worry. Those things define us. We
can also hold on to faith, our loved ones, and integrity. These also define
us, and the legacy is passed down.

When we get to the end of our days, may our legacy be that we lived
like Jesus.

> ### Come With Me
> *It's not my desire
> that anything have a
> hold on your heart.*

PUSH OUT DEEPER: Luke 9:23–25; 2 Thessalonians 1:11;
1 Corinthians 13:13; Psalm 37:23

Unashamed

"If anyone is ashamed of me and my message, the Son of Man
will be ashamed of that person when he returns in his glory and
in the glory of the Father and the holy angels."

LUKE 9:26 NLT

THERE ARE LOTS of opportunities for Jesus to be embarrassed by
his disciples, but he never is. Where others see a fumble, he sees
a teaching moment. Where others see their roughhewn state, he sees
their hearts.

Neither are they ashamed of Jesus. He's without sin. He's perfect. Yet
he's ostracized by people in power. The disciples stand by his side no
matter what others think.

Shame is stealthy. We would never turn our
backs on Jesus, but shame tells us to silence his
message. It's too old-fashioned. It's counter-
cultural. Surely we can live a good life and keep
quiet about Jesus.

> **Come With Me**
> *What will the world hear
> when you speak of me?*

What if we stood up for Jesus the way he stands up for us?

We'd scatter shame to the winds. We'd tell the world that he's our
Savior. We'd tell anyone who will listen that it's impossible to be embarrassed of a gospel that so utterly saves us.

PUSH OUT DEEPER: Luke 9:25–27; 1 John 5:9; John 5:32; Daniel 3:18

Shekinah Glory

While Jesus was praying, the appearance of his face changed, and his clothes became dazzling white. Suddenly, both Moses and Elijah were talking with him.

LUKE 9:29–30 GW

MOSES AND ELIJAH APPEAR in a blaze of glory, similar to super-heroes appearing on the scene. Moses once pointed a rod over the Red Sea, and it parted. Elijah was whisked away in a whirlwind to heaven.

The disciples are in awe, but then they notice Jesus.

The *Shekinah* glory on Jesus' face speaks of two worlds—one in which the disciples exist, and one Jesus calls home. They witness a monumental event as the old covenant fades to the new. Moses represents the law and Elijah the prophets. Jesus stands between them, symbolizing a new agreement between God and man.

The New Covenant demolished every barrier between man and God.

Too many live under the old covenant. We hold up our list of rules and try to live by them. We bring our sacrifices and wonder if it's enough. We wait for someone more holy to speak to God on our behalf.

Come With Me
My covenant of mercy is for you today.

In the New Covenant, our commandment is to love God and others. He doesn't want our sacrifices, but our love. No boundaries separate us from God.

The New Covenant represents his glory, but it's our glorious invitation.

PUSH OUT DEEPER: Luke 9:29–31; 2 Kings 2:1–11; Exodus 14:21–25; Hebrews 8:6

Exodus

> They were glorious to see. And they were speaking about his exodus from this world, which was about to be fulfilled in Jerusalem.
>
> LUKE 9:31 NLT

THE DISCIPLES WAKE UP to a dazzling light, like lightning. Two men are posted, one on each side of Jesus. They can't hear what they are saying, but they know it's spectacular.

Jesus will soon leave the earth.

His glory will stutter and his light will dim for three days. He'll rise and his light will explode with brilliance.

Later, when the disciples peer into an empty tomb, they'll recall his glory.

They'll talk about his shining face.

They'll marvel at what they didn't understand.

They'll remember the moment they were asleep and Jesus' glory woke them up.

Jesus calls the church to wake up! Our sleeping faith veils his glory. It's not departed. We've just failed to see it. It's been there all along.

Father, open our eyes. Rouse us from our slumber. We desire to wake up to the majesty of Christ, risen and alive.

> **Come With Me**
> *My glory is greater than the glimmer you've experienced. Let me show you who I am.*

PUSH OUT DEEPER: Luke 9:31–32; Ezekiel 3:23; Acts 7:55; Ezekiel 1:28

Monuments

As Moses and Elijah were starting to leave, Peter, not even knowing what he was saying, blurted out, "Master, it's wonderful for us
to be here! Let's make three shelters as memorials—one for you,
one for Moses, and one for Elijah."

LUKE 9:33 NLT

JOSHUA SET UP A MONUMENT by an oak tree. Jacob built a pillar
and poured oil over it. Samuel set up a stone between Mizpah and
Shen and called it Ebenezer. Each memorialized a special meeting between God and man.

Peter wants to build three memorials—one for Elijah, one for Moses,
and one for Jesus—but Jesus won't have it. His
greatest feat isn't standing between two fathers of
the faith. It will be hanging between two thieves
on a cross.

> **Come With Me**
> *Don't let the glory of
> the past keep you from
> stepping into the new.*

When we experience a high in God, we are
tempted to linger in the glory days. We reminisce
about the old days when God did this or that. We
hang on to the past, when God has something brand-new.

These are important monuments in our faith, but his redeeming
work continues.

We'll thank him for the glory days but we keep moving. We'll celebrate
what God has done but look toward what is to come. The miracles of the past
are stepping-stones, not a stone wall to keep us from discovering the new.

PUSH OUT DEEPER: Luke 9:33–36; Genesis 28:11; 2 John 1:5; Isaiah 43:18–19

Are You Listening?

"Let these words sink into your ears: The Son of Man is about to be delivered into the hands of men."

LUKE 9:44 ESV

JESUS AND HIS MEN spend a few days in the holy place of transfiguration. When they come down from the mountain, they are immediately met by a father and his only son. The boy is writhing in distress.

Jesus heals him and gives him back to his father.

He tells a story of another Father and Son. In the not-too-distant future, the Son will be delivered into the hands of angry men. He will suffer for a while, but then be delivered back into the loving hands of his heavenly Father.

He tells the disciples this message three times in three different ways, but they don't understand.

He'll tell them again and again until they do.

We see his miracles. We read his Word. We experience his presence. Even with these blessings, there are times we don't hear what God is trying to say. He speaks, but our part is to listen. When we don't understand, we go back and we listen again.

> ### Come With Me
> Yes, that's me speaking to you. I'll say it as many ways as is needed until you know it's me.

He's patient with us. He'll speak it in as many ways as is needed, until we understand.

PUSH OUT DEEPER: Luke 9:37–45; Matthew 11:5; Revelation 2:7; Revelation 3:6

Oh So Human

> An argument started among the disciples as to which of them would be the greatest.
>
> LUKE 9:46 NIV

IT'S AN OLD ARGUMENT between the disciples as they push and shove for position. Jesus overhears their conversation and perceives the motivation behind the argument. He reaches for a child and pulls the child close to his side.

Whoever welcomes a little child like this welcomes me.

Whoever welcomes me welcomes my heavenly Father who sent me.

He's the King of Kings, but his position resembles nothing of an earthly king. There isn't a throne. There is no gold or jewels. No slaves. No luxuries. As a king, he deems the least of these to be the greatest treasure.

> **Come With Me**
>
> *Every time you love the least of these, you love me.*

So which of the disciples is the greatest? The one who notices the least among them. The one who doesn't parade around as the most important.

Faith isn't positioning for personal favor, but a posture of serving.

When we welcome the unnoticed, the uninvited—those our society calls the least—into our midst, we serve alongside our King of Kings.

PUSH OUT DEEPER: Luke 9:46–48; Exodus 22:22; Deuteronomy 10:18; Psalm 68:5

Together We're Better

John said to Jesus, "Master, we saw someone using your name
to cast out demons, but we told him to stop because he isn't in
our group."

LUKE 9:49 NLT

WHEN JOHN SEES A GROUP of people using Jesus' name to
cast out demons, his first reaction is anger. He is so distracted
that they aren't in his club that he fails to notice those who are set free.

Notice the chasm in the beautiful body of Christ.

We divide by denomination. By creed. By culture. By race. It's confusing to a watching world as believers divide over minute differences, instead of linking arms around a common love for Jesus.

It's an age-old trap of the enemy. He divides God's people to distract them from the call to "go."

What if we banded together? One race holding hands with the other. Denominations working side by side. Ministries looking out for the ministry across the street, or across the world. Our common ground is Jesus.

> **Come With Me**
> *The church is diverse.
> It's beautiful. Step
> across that dividing
> line and grab a
> believer by the hand.*

The work is far from complete, and the need is great.

Savior, we are better together. Smash down the walls that divide us. We pray for that church across town. We pray for that ministry. We pray for that believer who may not look like us, but who is our brother or sister. May the church come together in your name.

PUSH OUT DEEPER: Luke 9:49–50; Colossians 2:19; Ephesians 4:16; Romans 12:4

Fiery

He sent messengers ahead of him. They went into a Samaritan village to arrange a place for him to stay. But the people didn't welcome him, because he was on his way to Jerusalem.

LUKE 9:52–53 GW

JAMES AND JOHN GO AHEAD to find lodging in the Samaritan city. They are turned away. They beg Jesus to call fire down from heaven and burn them all to ashes. He turns them down immediately. Jesus didn't come to cause division, but to bring men into unity with God. He didn't come to harm, but to heal.

Personal rejection fires up all kinds of emotions. The first reaction may be to give the offender what they deserve. They made us feel bad, so we offer a fiery response.

Rejection of our Savior may feel just as wrong. We may be tempted to call down fire in our conversations or interactions with unbelievers.

Our passion is a gift from God, and when aimed in the right direction it produces good work. When that same passion is released for harm, it burns the bridges we've so carefully built.

> ### Come With Me
> Your feelings are not wrong. It's what you do with them that matters.

Jesus, turn our passion in the right direction. Thank you that we feel everything, beautiful and otherwise. You are our safe place to share those feelings. May our words be fired with wisdom and lead the way to you.

PUSH OUT DEEPER: Luke 9:52–56; Proverbs 15:18; Proverbs 25:15; Proverbs 15:1

Harder Paths

And Jesus said to him, "Foxes have holes and birds of the air have nests, but the Son of Man has nowhere to lay His head."

LUKE 9:58 NKJV

JESUS IS APPROACHED by those who desire to join the team. Jesus reminds the first that following him isn't a road of comfort. He asks the second to attend to the living instead of the dead. To the third he explains that following him will lead away from what feels like home.

Jesus refuses to entice them into something that seems intriguing from the outside but which requires real sacrifice behind the scenes.

Loving Jesus is an amazing adventure, but it's not without cost.

Faith is joy and sacrifice.

We climb spiritual hills that take our breath away. We lift our hands in adoration. We experience moments of glory.

We do hard things. We climb out of our comfort zone. We forgive. We believe his Word is true, even as we wait for an answer.

> ### Come With Me
> *Walking with me will lead you up harder paths, but that is where you and I will meet most closely.*

Faith is sweet dependence on Jesus. It's familiarity. In the harder paths, he shows us where to go and what to do.

We count the cost and know it's worth it. The price Jesus paid is far more than we'll ever invest.

PUSH OUT DEEPER: Luke 9:57–62; Psalm 18:2; Proverbs 18:10; 2 Samuel 22:2

Two by Two

The Lord now chose seventy-two other disciples and sent them ahead in pairs to all the towns and places he planned to visit.

LUKE 10:1 NLT

THE DISCIPLES AND JESUS have simply traveled from place to place. Now there's a new strategy. Jesus chooses seventy-two from among his growing group of supporters and sends them out, two by two. They will go ahead of Jesus. They'll branch out into every town and to all the places he plans to visit in the future. This region is vast and untapped. With the new plan, no one will be missed.

Just as Jesus commissioned the seventy-two disciples, we have a heavenly assignment. Nearly sixty-five hundred people groups exist who don't know about the love of Jesus.

> ## Come With Me
> *Going isn't a place; it's readiness to partner with me, whatever that might look like. Some go. Some help others go.*

The need is vast, and the mission to rescue God's people has not gone away. God desires to draw every one of them into the fold to call them son or daughter.

He sends us out, one by one, two by two, thousands upon thousands, to draw them home.

Will we go?

PUSH OUT DEEPER: Luke 10:1–2; Matthew 10:1; Isaiah 43:6; Jeremiah 31:8–9

Harvest

These were his instructions to them: "The harvest is great, but the workers are few. So pray to the Lord who is in charge of the harvest; ask him to send more workers into his fields."

LUKE 10:2 NLT

WHEN JESUS SENDS OUT the seventy-two, there is no sign of a harvest. There is no sign of seeds sprouting.

There's only fallow ground.

Jesus envisioned the fruit long before the harvest was a possibility.

When Jesus sends us out, he doesn't see it the way we do. He sees the possibility in that untilled ground. He imagines that seed of faith dropped into a ministry or that person. He sees how obedience, even when it appears that nothing is happening, fertilizes and waters and nourishes that seed.

> ## Come With Me
> *What you see as impossible I see as a potential harvest.*

Let's imagine the harvest as he does. See that fallow ground rich with fruit. See that sinner as a miracle waiting to happen. See that ministry that impacted one—and how that one will impact generations.

He casts the vision.

We plant the seed.

Together, there is a harvest.

PUSH OUT DEEPER: Luke 10:1–3; John 4:35; Mark 4:29; John 15:8

I Send You

Go your ways: behold, I send you.

LUKE 10:3 KJV

THE EMPHASIS IS NOT on who is being sent, but the Sender. This completely shifts the burden from the seventy-two disciples to Jesus. He knows where they are going. He understands the size of the job. He is aware of the hurdles, but also of the possibilities.

How many times do we look at a God-sized task and react with worry? That worry influences our words. Our words crop up in our outlook. Our outlook paralyzes us and we are stuck.

Let's take the pressure off. He sees further down the road than we do. What we may view as prospective failure he sees as potential victory. What we imagine as too big to tackle he sees as every believer fitting in the overall plan.

> ## Come With Me
> Don't overthink the adventure. Play your part; I'll play mine.

He sends us. All he asks is that we go.

Lord, we won't ask you to reduce the size of the task, but ask you to reduce the size of our worry. If you send us, you'll equip us. Teach us what we need to know. Beyond that, we trust your guidance and your word.

PUSH OUT DEEPER: Luke 10:1–3; Exodus 4:10; Acts 7:22; Philippians 1:6

As a Lamb

"Go your way; behold, I am sending you out as lambs in the midst of wolves."

LUKE 10:3 ESV

JESUS SENDS OUT the seventy-two disciples as lambs in the midst of wolves. This sounds frightening, but Jesus isn't saying they'll be ripped apart. Rather, he's teaching them how to overcome hostile territory, just as he does.

Jesus came to earth as a lamb among wolves. They were hostile and unwilling to receive him.

Jesus persuaded with gentleness rather than unrestrained power. He spoke truth, always motivated by love. His countenance was gentle and humble, even as he exuded strength. Jesus lifted people up rather than put them down, even when he was outnumbered or overwhelmed.

> ### Come With Me
> *You are my lamb and I am your Shepherd. I'll protect you as you go out among the wolves.*

That portrait of gentle strength is our greatest inspiration.

Our strongest move is to disarm rather than to destroy. We have a message to share, and we don't dilute it. Our approach is as a lamb among wolves. As we approach that person or situation with gentle strength, it's our strongest move.

PUSH OUT DEEPER: Luke 10:3–4; John 1:29; 1 Peter 1:9; 1 Peter 3:8

Peace

"Whatever house you enter, first say, 'Peace be to this house!' And
if a son of peace is there, your peace will rest upon him. But if
not, it will return to you."

LUKE 10:5–6 ESV

"PEACE BE TO THIS HOUSE" is a typical Aramaic saying announcing blessing over everyone who lives under a roof. Even if the blessing is not received, the disciples will walk away with peace intact.

When our goal is to bestow peace from the very beginning, it's never in vain. Peace refuses to stir up greater discord. Peace opens the door for resolution or conversation. When we approach in peace, we come with the best intentions. If our words of peace are refused, we keep moving toward Jesus, rather than toward drama or heated arguments that only cause additional damage. When our words are bathed in peace, even if nothing works the way we hoped it might, Jesus reigns.

> ### Come With Me
> *You can't change the way another person feels, but how you approach them will leave either peace or discord as a result.*

Jesus, help us remove the chip from our shoulder. Adjust our attitude. If conflict occurs, we can deal with it with your help. Let our first words be filled with peace. Let us walk away in peace.

PUSH OUT DEEPER: Luke 10:4–9; 1 Peter 4:14; 1 Samuel 16:4; Exodus 18:7

Rejected

> Then he said to the disciples, "Anyone who accepts your message is also accepting me. And anyone who rejects you is rejecting me. And anyone who rejects me is rejecting God, who sent me."
>
> LUKE 10:16 NLT

NO ONE LIKES TO BE REJECTED, not even the disciples. When the crowd rejects the disciples, they reject Jesus. When they reject Jesus, they reject the gift he desires to give. When they reject the gift, they reject Jehovah God.

This rejection will lead to heartache for generations of God's people. He will reach for them, and they will choose less than God's best, over and over again. They will worship idols when a loving God waits with open arms.

When the seventy-two disciples brave this unknown region, their message is not rejected. Wonders and healings take place as a result.

What is the difference?

God's beloved—and we are all his beloved—chose to receive the invitation.

> **Come With Me**
>
> *I have so much to show you. There is more to discover as we walk together.*

This invitation still stands. Every word is true. He invites us to live, breathe, and move as his people. There are many who will reject that message, but let us reach to receive him with every fiber of our being.

PUSH OUT DEEPER: Luke 10:12–16; Ephesians 1:3; Matthew 7:11; Isaiah 63:7

Falling From Heaven

Jesus said to them, "I watched Satan fall from heaven like lightning."

LUKE 10:18 GW

THE SEVENTY-TWO MINISTER in the Gentile districts. As they talk with people and move from one part of the region to the next, they see only the short-term impact. They see one convert or one prayer or one potential church plant.

Jesus saw the long-term impact as they crossed into the enemy's territory. Satan was firmly entrenched and thought he had won. As the seventy-two talked with one after another, the enemy was shaken from his throne. Principalities and powers shuddered as men, women, and children believed in the name of Jesus!

> **Come With Me**
>
> *I can't wait to show you what transpired because of your faithfulness.*

Lord, help us not be shortsighted.

Ministry is more than what the eye can see. We see one convert, when God sees thousands over time. We see one prayer, while God sees the eternal impact. We are limited in what we see, while God scans eternity for the fruit of faithfulness, heaping, poured out, showered, and lavished.

One day we'll stand before our Savior. He'll take us by the hand and show how faithfulness shook Satan from his throne like lightning. He'll reveal how one act, one word, one response of yes reached farther than we can imagine.

PUSH OUT DEEPER: Luke 10:17–19; Psalm 51:10; Ephesians 2:10; Matthew 25:21

Deep, Legitimate Joy

"Nevertheless do not rejoice in this, that the spirits are subject to you, but rather rejoice because your names are written in heaven."

LUKE 10:20 NKJV

THERE ARE UPS AND DOWNS to following Jesus. If disciples live by their emotions, spiritual stability is flung out the door. They'll stand on the mountaintop one day and at the bottom of the sea the next. Jesus asks the disciples to tether their joy to the unmovable. It can't be taken from them. It's not tied to emotions. It isn't dependent upon a person.

Rejoice, for your names are written in heaven.

There's deep, legitimate joy to be found in this assurance.

We celebrate good things that come our way. We celebrate the ups. We laugh and gather with others. These are truly blessings, but our unmovable truth is that our names are written in heaven. We will spend eternity with him.

Heaven is our promise. That's our assurance.

That's deep, legitimate joy that cannot be shaken.

> ### Come With Me
> *On the day you first followed me, your name was written in heaven.*

PUSH OUT DEEPER: Luke 10:19–20; John 14:1–3; Revelation 20:12; Hebrews 12:23

90

How Blessed We Are

He turned to his disciples in private and said to them, "How blessed you are to see what you've seen."

LUKE 10:23 GW

THE PROPHETS OF OLD understood that deliverance was coming, but they didn't get to see it. Jewish forefathers cried out that a Messiah would come. They watched as priests went into the Holy of Holies. They prayed one day to see him up close and personal.

God longs to commune with his people. He sent Jesus to shatter the distance.

The disciples participated in that long-awaited miracle. They witnessed the supernatural as the Messiah walked the earth. They stood front and center as prophecies unfolded. They partnered with God himself in the unveiling of the New Covenant.

How blessed they were to be a part of such a historical and spiritual revelation. How blessed we are!

Jesus tore the veil that kept us at a distance. No barriers exist between us and God. We feel his presence. Not only were our sins carried upon Jesus on the cross, but we can take them to him every single day.

How blessed we are to walk freely into the presence of God. There is no barrier, for Jesus became the sacrifice that brought us back together.

> **Come With Me**
> As you accept my sacrifice, you become a part of the miracle.

PUSH OUT DEEPER: Luke 10:22–24; 2 Corinthians 3:16; John 3:16–17; Isaiah 9:6

Heart Check

> But he wanted to justify himself, so he asked Jesus, "And who is my neighbor?"
>
> LUKE 10:29 NIV

A LAWYER ASKED how to inherit eternal life. It's a conversation that arises often among religious scholars. They debate on how to get to heaven, but also how to live a life that is rich and full and pleases God.

Jesus replies with the letter of the law: Love God with all your heart, soul, and mind, and love your neighbor.

The lawyer asks Jesus to define his neighbor. Perhaps it is the person who lives next door, or across the street. Maybe it's the one who sits next to him in the temple.

Jesus takes the conversation from theological to personal. The lawyer wanted a checklist, but Jesus desires to give him a heart check.

Living a sermon is vastly different from hearing a sermon.

> **Come With Me**
> *You've heard it. Are you willing to live a rich and full life?*

Hearing it inspires. Living it moves us from inspiration to perspiration. Rather than rules to follow, faith becomes a lifestyle. We love God with all of our heart, soul, and mind. We love him because he's worthy of loving.

We love our neighbor. Not just the family next door, but the people God places in our path. We open our busy lives to community.

That's sold-out faith. It's living a life that is rich and full, and that pleases God.

PUSH OUT DEEPER: Luke 10:25–30; Leviticus 19:18; John 13:34; Galatians 5:14

Good Neighbor

"Going over to him, the Samaritan soothed his wounds with olive oil and wine and bandaged them. Then he put the man on his own donkey and took him to an inn, where he took care of him."

LUKE 10:34 NLT

A MAN IS ROBBED, stripped, and left on the side of the road. He's bleeding and half-dead. Two people pass by, almost as if he's invisible. They keep going.

A third man comes on the scene, a Samaritan. He kneels beside him to bandage his wounds. He takes the wounded man into town and pays for him to stay in a safe place.

They were all neighbors, but only one acted as a neighbor.

Serving as a neighbor isn't defined by location. A neighbor might be the stranger at the convenience store or the family that just moved across the street. It's not limited by race or age or economic status.

> **Come With Me**
> *On-purpose love changes you and changes the world around you.*

We discover the identity of our neighbor as we *become* a neighbor.

When we act neighborly, we act as a potential friend. Our words and actions leave an impression not soon forgotten.

Who is our neighbor?

It's that one God places in our path and to whom we show kindness.

PUSH OUT DEEPER: Luke 10:31–37; Romans 13:8–10; Colossians 3:12–14; Ephesians 5:1

Hardworking

She had a sister called Mary, who sat at the Lord's feet listening
to what he said.

LUKE 10:39 NIV

MARTHA OWNS THE HOUSE, and her sister, Mary, lives with
her. The house is filled with guests. Martha scurries from one
task to another. She checks the food. She whisks from room to room,
ensuring every detail is in place.

When she finds her sister sitting at Jesus' feet, she's irritated. There's
too much to do. She's also vexed at her friend Jesus.

Can't you see how hard I'm working? Why don't you tell Mary to help me?

Martha wants to please Jesus, and she is doing what she knows how.
But she is so busy doing things *for* Jesus that she almost misses being
with him.

God doesn't require perfection. He doesn't
demand that we work incessantly to please him.
Sometimes we are so tuned in to perfection that
a ministry or an event becomes tedious rather
than enjoyable.

> **Come With Me**
> *Put aside your schedule
> and sit with me.*

We can be so busy doing things for Jesus that we miss being with him.

The real sacrifice in our culture is ditching busyness to spend time
with Jesus.

We will always have tasks to perform, but loving Jesus isn't one of
them.

PUSH OUT DEEPER: Luke 10:38–42; Hosea 6:6; John 11:5; Exodus 33:7–11

One Thing

> "There is only one thing worth being concerned about. Mary has discovered it, and it will not be taken away from her."
>
> LUKE 10:42 NLT

THE FOOD IS PUT AWAY. Neighbors have departed. The night sky darkens and bed beckons. A weary Martha falls into bed. When she wakes up the next day, she'll repeat many of the same tasks.

So much of what we accomplish is short-lived. Laundry is washed and gets dirty again. A meal is prepared, and another will be cooked the next day. We meet deadlines, only to have another slide onto our desk. Taxes are turned in, but they are due again the next year.

The one thing that isn't short-lived is what we store in our hearts.

His Word takes root. His promises are unchanging. His teaching is timeless. His faithful words hold us when life turns upside-down. There are many things that consume our time, but there is only one thing that is lasting. The power of the Word over our hearts can never be undone.

Come With Me

I see that you are pulled in a thousand different ways. Stay with me, if only for a moment.

PUSH OUT DEEPER: Luke 10:40–42; Psalm 106:48; Psalm 90:2; Psalm 93:2

Teach Me

Once Jesus was praying in a certain place. When he stopped praying, one of his disciples said to him, "Lord, teach us to pray as John taught his disciples."

LUKE 11:1 GW

JESUS OFTEN PRAYED. The disciples see him come out of his prayer times empowered and refueled.

They want that too. They want that heavenly connection!

When we see others who seem to have a one-to-one relationship with God, we may wonder if it's only for the special people—like John the Baptist.

It's for all of us. Prayer is a conversation. As we talk, he listens. He's not looking at credentials, but at our desire to know him.

We don't put a timer on our conversations. We walk in with no other agenda but to be with him. The longer we pray this way, the more ingrained it becomes.

Our ongoing prayer with our heavenly Father influences others. A child notices that we take our worries to prayer and leave a burden behind. A friend feels strengthened when we petition God for her sake. A loved one is encouraged when we take him by the hand and pray. Prayer changes us. It also draws in those who long for the same connection with God.

Come With Me

Prayer changes you, but it also ripples far beyond our conversation to touch the lives of others.

PUSH OUT DEEPER: Luke 11:1–4; James 5:16; Colossians 4:2; Luke 9:18

Hallowed

He said to them, "When you pray, say: "'Father, hallowed be your name, your kingdom come.'""

LUKE 11:2 NIV

THE DISCIPLES KNOW the words to say. They know the cadence in which to say them. They don't want one more formula on *how* to pray, but to know God.

Holy is your name.

He is holy. We enter a sacred place as we whisper those words.

Come With Me

*I am a holy God,
and I am your God.*

We acknowledge *who* he is: our holy God.

We acknowledge *what* he is: holy.

Sacred. Divine. Revered. Mighty!

We are enclosed in a holy place as we pray, whether thanking him for our food or crying out for help. We may not have the most articulate words, but that's okay.

Save me.

Help me.

Thank you.

Show me the next step.

Our first move toward prayer is to simply move toward our holy God.

PUSH OUT DEEPER: Luke 11:1–4; Jeremiah 29:12; Jeremiah 33:3; Acts 16:25

Waltz

"Forgive us our sins, as we forgive those who sin against us. And don't let us yield to temptation."

LUKE 11:4 NLT

FORGIVING IS A GRACE-FILLED MOVE, like a waltz.

We receive it. We give it.

If we receive forgiveness but fail to extend it to others, we stumble. Bitterness leaves little room for grace. It halts the rhythm of our faith.

We may struggle to accept forgiveness because we don't feel we deserve it.

Yet isn't that grace?

We choose a grudge over forgiving others because they don't deserve it.

But isn't that grace?

Forgiveness demolishes strongholds in the heart of a believer. We are free to leave behind resentment. We are free to release long-held animosity.

Isn't that the fruit of a grace-filled life?

Jesus, forgive us our sins as we forgive others. We've held on to resentment for too long. When we confess, you help us to clean up our messes. You are honest about our mistakes, but grace-filled. Show us how to forgive like you.

> ### Come With Me
> *Surrender those feelings every day, and one day they'll no longer hold you captive.*

PUSH OUT DEEPER: Luke 11:1–4; James 2:13; Matthew 5:7; James 3:17

Ask, Seek, Knock

"And I tell you, ask, and it will be given to you; seek, and you will find; knock, and it will be opened to you."

LUKE 11:9 ESV

GUESTS ARE COMING, and there's no bread in the house. It's late, but he knocks on his neighbor's door anyway. There's no answer, but he keeps knocking. Finally, the neighbor comes to the door and gives him what he needs.

Is God that sleeping neighbor? Do we need to bang on the door relentlessly to wake him up?

Never!

Jesus often told parables to contrast a truth. He does so in this parable. The sleeping neighbor is the reverse of our heavenly Father. God never slumbers, nor is he deaf to our call for help.

> **Come With Me**
>
> *Child, I heard you from the very first knock. I'm coming.*

Yet let's look at the man in need of bread. He immediately goes for help. He isn't afraid to present his need. He remains until he receives his answer.

Jesus shows us how to pray: Ask. Seek. Knock.

Ask: Invite God into the middle of a struggle from the beginning.

Seek: Look to God always. He's awake in the middle of the night. The answer might take time, but stay close to God while you wait.

Knock: As we pray, he hears. He answers, according to his will. We can trust he hears that knock, and wants the very best for us.

PUSH OUT DEEPER: Luke 11:5–9; Romans 8:26; 1 Thessalonians 5:17; Jude 1:20

Good Gift

"Which of you fathers, if your son asks for a fish, will give him
a snake instead?"

LUKE 11:11 NIV

MOST FATHERS WOULDN'T give a snake to a child who asked for a fish. They wouldn't give a scorpion if asked for an egg. If an earthly father, altogether human and living in a fallen world, knows how to give good gifts to his children, how much greater does our heavenly Father give to those who ask?

When we ask, seek, and knock, the Holy Spirit opens the door and welcomes us in. He knows the heart of the Father regarding us, and he knows our intentions. He is our Counselor. He is our comfort. He provides discernment and direction when we don't know whom to trust or where to go.

The person of the Holy Spirit is woven into our relationship with God. He's been there since the beginning. When we cried out to Abba Father, we received his Spirit as well. Our earthly fathers give gifts as they know how, but our heavenly Father has given us the greatest gift.

> ## Come With Me
> *When you don't know what to say or do, sit quietly. The Holy Spirit will shift the focus from your struggle to me, and you'll find what you need.*

PUSH OUT DEEPER: Luke 11:10–13; James 4:3; Matthew 6:6; John 14:16

Evidence

One day Jesus cast out a demon from a man who couldn't speak, and when the demon was gone, the man began to speak. The crowds were amazed, but some of them said, "No wonder he can cast out demons. He gets his power from Satan, the prince of demons."

LUKE 11:14–15 NLT

THE TIDE IS TURNING from popularity to extreme scrutiny. When Jesus heals a man silenced by a demon, the majority are in awe. Some spread lies, however, saying Jesus gets his power from the prince of demons. Such an accusation stirs confusion. Is this miracle from God? Is it from Beelzebub, an evil angel found in old traditions?

As they argue, the man who just received his voice is forgotten. If only they'd take a second look. The evidence is in the miracle, but they miss it.

> **Come With Me**
> *Do you remember that miracle? Let's celebrate again over that gift.*

Miracles are unfolding even now because of Jesus.

Somewhere a woman was just cleansed of her sin. Somewhere a son just knelt in desperation and was delivered from addiction. Miracles are taking place in families, within relationships, in financial needs, and in the heart of that prodigal child.

Where does Jesus get his power?

The evidence is in the miracles.

PUSH OUT DEEPER: Luke 11:14–16; Job 16:3; 2 Timothy 2:14; Philippians 4:9

Stronger

"When a strong man, fully armed, guards his own mansion, his property is safe."

LUKE 11:21 GW

THE STRONG MAN'S WEAPONS are ready as he guards his property. Until another man comes who is bigger and stronger. Then the strong man is overpowered; his weapons are taken. His property is gone!

Consider the man oppressed by the demon. He was imprisoned and unable to free himself until Jesus—bigger and stronger than the enemy—fought for him and won. Jesus reclaimed him, for he never rightfully belonged to the enemy.

> **Come With Me**
>
> *It may appear that the enemy has staked his claim, but I am working on that loved one's behalf. I'm coming to reclaim my own.*

A house divided against itself cannot stand.

Evil will never be the instrument of virtue. Virtue will never lead to evil.

If we ever struggle to know who is behind that thought or desire, we can trust in this: Our Savior will never open the door and wave us into a relationship, a place, a way of thinking that allows the enemy to stake a claim.

The enemy will never release, save, or attempt to rescue us.

We always know whom to trust.

It's our God, bigger and stronger, the one who reclaims what is rightfully his.

PUSH OUT DEEPER: Luke 11:17–23; Romans 8:31; 1 John 5:4; 1 Corinthians 15:57

Emptied

"And when he comes, he finds it swept and put in order."

LUKE 11:25 NKJV

THE MAN ONCE BELEAGUERED by demons has been emptied. His heart has been swept clean. Every corner. Every hidden place. He's a vessel waiting to be filled.

Jesus issues a warning to him and to those within earshot.

Demons are restless. They will return to see if there's a vacancy.

When a believer is filled with the presence and power of Jesus, demons will be met with a No Vacancy sign.

> ### Come With Me
> *My living water is endless, pouring over you day by day. I'll fill those empty places with my Spirit.*

The man is empty, but Jesus promised to fill him with good.

Has Jesus swept away our sin? Has he emptied us of the baggage we once carried in our thoughts? Has he cleansed every nook and cranny? Are we a vessel waiting to be filled?

When we've been emptied, it's time to fill up.

Jesus offers living water to pour over those empty places. His presence saturates. The power of the Holy Spirit overflows in us and through us as we live by the Spirit.

The enemy may roam to and fro, seeking whom he may devour. But when we are filled with living water, there is no room for him at all.

PUSH OUT DEEPER: Luke 11:24–26; John 7:37; Matthew 23:27; Revelation 21:6

Blessing Upon Blessing

He replied, "Blessed rather are those who hear the word of God and obey it."

LUKE 11:28 NIV

ONE WOMAN IS SO OVERCOME by what she just witnessed—the healing of the demoniac—that she shouts out!

"Blessed is your mother. Blessed is her womb. Blessed is she that nursed you."

She sees Mary as special because she's the parent of such an important man.

Jesus answers softly.

Blessed rather are those who hear the word of God and obey it.

Certainly Mary is blessed, but not because she has a prominent son. She's blessed because she hears the Word of God and obeys it. She's blessed because she is loved by God almighty. This is the blessing that will hold her close on the day her son is crucified. It is the blessing that will keep her in the days he is in the tomb. It will surround and flow through her when he is risen.

> **Come With Me**
> *It's not who you know,*
> *but whose you are.*

Our greatest blessings are not tied to whom we know or what we do or how important anyone believes us to be. Our blessing upon blessing is found as we hear the Word of God and obey it and call ourselves children of God.

PUSH OUT DEEPER: Luke 11:27–28; Acts 15:7; Matthew 13:16; 1 Peter 1:8

A Sign

"The queen from the south will stand up at the time of judgment with the men who live today. She will condemn them, because she came from the ends of the earth to hear Solomon's wisdom. But look, someone greater than Solomon is here!"

LUKE 11:31 GW

THE CROWD HAS BEEN GRANTED SIGNS as big as billboards. They've witnessed miracles! They want one more sign. His deity couldn't be more obvious if a spotlight from heaven shone on him, but they are blind.

They see but don't believe.

If the prophets of old were to appear in the room, there might be real drama. They'd soundly condemn the crowd for missing the utmost sign. Jesus is standing right in front of them.

Come With Me
If you can't see, ask me and I'll open your spiritual eyes.

A man has been made whole right in front of them!

Do we ask for a sign?

He's right in front of us. His Word leaps from the pages of the Bible to speak to us. His death and resurrection stand as proof of his love.

The sign we seek is right in front of us as we open our spiritual eyes.

PUSH OUT DEEPER: Luke 11:30–32; Luke 11:16; John 1:1; John 1:14

No Part Dark

"If then your whole body is full of light, having no part dark, it will be wholly bright, as when a lamp with its rays gives you light."

LUKE 11:36 ESV

JOSHUA, THE SON OF NUN, stepped into leadership when filled with the Spirit. Bezalel, son of Uri, was spurred to the highest level of creativity when filled with the Spirit. He was known as a man of wisdom, understanding, knowledge, and the highest workmanship.

Then there was King Saul. He relied on his own power, and the Spirit of the Lord departed from him.

Do we understand the gift that is given and how it transforms us?

> **Come With Me**
> *Bring to life the Spirit that is in you through belief. It's for you too.*

As we embrace that power, he becomes a light that reflects like a beacon on a hill. No matter how bleak or dark a place or situation may be, that light transcends in us.

PUSH OUT DEEPER: Luke 11:33–36; Numbers 27:18; 1 Samuel 16:14; Exodus 31:1–3

Alms Giving

"But now as for what is inside you—be generous to the poor, and everything will be clean for you."

LUKE 11:41 NIV

THE HOST REPRIMANDS JESUS IN FRONT OF EVERYONE. *You haven't washed.*

It's not that Jesus came to the table with dirty hands, but that he didn't wash his hands all the way to the elbow. Pharisees are known for taking simple guidelines and making them complicated. Even if a person performs to the letter of the law, it might not be to a Pharisee's specification.

They demand public conformity, even as many of them privately sin. Jesus exposes the falsehood of performing charitable acts only for show. He explains that if a person is spotless on the outside but filled with sinful pride, he's lost his way.

> **Come With Me**
> *Your greatest battles are in private, and so are your greatest triumphs.*

We can pretend to be good and miss God's goodness. Our heavenly Father isn't as concerned with who we are in public nearly as much as who we are when no one is looking. When we seek to honor him privately, the need for guidelines falls away.

We obey, not to please anyone else, but out of our love for him.

We are the same, no matter where we are.

PUSH OUT DEEPER: Luke 11:37–41; 1 Corinthians 13:4; Matthew 6:1–4; John 12:43

Rule Followers

"But woe to you Pharisees! For you tithe mint and rue and every herb, and neglect justice and the love of God. These you ought to have done, without neglecting the others."

LUKE 11:42 ESV

THE TITHE MAINTAINS THE TEMPLE, takes care of the priests, and cares for the poor, widowed, and orphaned. If the religious pay attention to how much they tithe but neglect or abuse people, what good is it?

Isn't it enough to follow the rules?

We can be rule followers or followers who respond generously. Rule followers give what they're supposed to, having done their duty.

There's little joy in such giving.

As generous believers, we look beyond the gift to the ones receiving it.

> **Come With Me**
> *When you give, your gift becomes an answer to prayer.*

A child is fed. A new believer receives a Bible of his very own. Ministries are launched and kingdom work spreads.

We get to be a part of that!

Giving isn't a rule to follow. It's a beautiful way to live.

PUSH OUT DEEPER: Luke 11:42–46; 2 Corinthians 9:6–9; 1 Timothy 6:18–19; Luke 3:11

Crossroads

> As he went away from there, the scribes and the Pharisees began
> to press him hard and to provoke him to speak about many things,
> lying in wait for him, to catch him in something he might say.
>
> LUKE 11:53–54 ESV

JESUS STEPS ON TOES OFTEN. He unveils insincerity, hypocrisy, and a lack of charity, especially in those who say they are religious. Conversations like these place the religious at a crossroads. They can keep doing what they are doing or choose another way.

The Pharisees and lawyers choose anger. They follow Jesus out of the house. They jostle him violently and try to provoke him.

If only Jesus would act as poorly as they, it might soothe their ruffled feelings.

When the Holy Spirit shows us areas where God wants to work, it puts us at a crossroads. It may be hard to hear. We can pretend we didn't hear. We can resist his gentle voice. We can put it off to another day.

If we desire to grow up in our faith, we take a different approach in that crossroads.

We surrender our work-in-progress life to him, and that's when real change begins.

Come With Me

When I show you an area that needs work, it's not a rebuke. It's to help you grow.

PUSH OUT DEEPER: Luke 11:47–54; Jeremiah 6:16; Isaiah 28:12; Ephesians 4:23

Like Leaven

"Whatever you have said in the dark will be heard in the daylight.
Whatever you have whispered in private rooms will be shouted
from the housetops."

LUKE 12:3 GW

HYPOCRISY WORKED ITS WAY into leadership like leaven in
dough, collapsing the Pharisees' moral and spiritual identity.
Hypocrites worked hard to hide their two-faced ways.

We might avoid talking about hypocrisy because it makes us feel
ashamed. Jesus wasn't afraid to talk about it. He came so that we might
live free. Rather than hide a struggle, we are invited to bring it into the
open and conquer it with his help.

Hypocrisy is similar to leading a double life. It's
saying one thing in public and another in private.
It's acting one way with a person, and differently
when they leave the room. We might feel guilty
if it is our battle, but what if we took the time to
uncover the source?

> **Come With Me**
> *If you've wronged
> another, do your best
> to make it right.*

Hypocrisy might be grounded in anger. It might be a need to express
how we feel without judgment. It could be jealousy.

Whatever the root cause, our God is willing to mend those broken
places. If we don't know what they are, he'll reveal them. As we become
whole on the inside, we don't have to pretend to be someone else on
the outside.

PUSH OUT DEEPER: Luke 12:1–3; Mark 12:15; Ephesians 4:25; 1 Peter 2:1

Misplaced Fear

Are not five sparrows sold for two farthings, and not one of them
is forgotten before God? But even the very hairs of your head
are all numbered. Fear not therefore: ye are of more value than
many sparrows.

LUKE 12:6–7 KJV

JESUS AND HIS MEN are pressed in by a multitude. They're man-
handled and the disciples are afraid. Jesus reminds them that man
can hurt their bodies, but cannot touch their souls.

Don't be afraid, not of these guys.

Fear of man is misplaced fear. Trust in God is never misplaced.

Man might try to take our good name, but God knows who we are.

He is sensitive to our worry. Not one of us is overlooked or forgotten, as he has painstakingly brushed every stroke and detail of our lives.

He has numbered every single hair on our head.

Come With Me
*I love you and am aware
of your fearful thoughts.
I am with you always.*

Man might try to knock us down, but God
picks us back up.

This God who notices the sparrow certainly
has us on his radar. When man strives to back us
into a corner, God sets us to flight with renewed
courage.

We don't have to fear man, whether against a multitude or in little things.
God frees us from the fear of man to operate in the courage of our Lord.

PUSH OUT DEEPER: Luke 12:4–7; Matthew 14:27; Proverbs 29:25; Psalm 118:6

Words Will Come

"And when they bring you before the synagogues and the rulers and the authorities, do not be anxious about how you should defend yourself or what you should say, for the Holy Spirit will teach you in that very hour what you ought to say."

LUKE 12:11–12 ESV

JESUS LEADS THE DISCIPLES from fear of people to awe of God. They will stand in front of hostile rulers and authorities, but the Holy Spirit will show them what to say. He asks them not to worry, for the words will come.

Criticism and unfair judgment are never welcome. Our instinct may be to craft a defense, even before there is a battle. We worry about what others are thinking or what they might say. This leads us to live on the defensive in our thoughts. This full-fledged mental battle is exhausting.

> ### Come With Me
> *Don't beat yourself up with anxious thoughts. We've got this.*

Let's put our defense strategies away. Open the door for the Counselor to come in. He will show us what to say. He'll tell us when we shouldn't speak. He slips into our anxious thoughts and makes himself at home. The Holy Spirit comforts and guides every disciple.

He'll be with us exactly when we need him.

PUSH OUT DEEPER: Luke 12:8–12; Exodus 4:12; 2 Timothy 4:17; Acts 6:10

Snare

> And he said to them, "Take care, and be on your guard against all covetousness, for one's life does not consist in the abundance of his possessions."
>
> LUKE 12:15 ESV

JESUS IS ASKED TO JUDGE an inheritance between brothers, but he refuses to entangle himself in the dispute. He quickly sees the real problem. This is a matter of covetousness, not fairness.

Jesus' concerns are always spiritual—preaching the gospel, bringing mankind back to God, tending to the sick and the lost. He doesn't wage war against governments. He doesn't step in to serve as a judge between parties over temporal matters.

> **Come With Me**
>
> *You are a fighter, but let it be for my purposes.*

We can easily get bogged down in disputes and fights, even those of others.

Our real battle is against an enemy who longs to separate humanity from God's love. We don't have time to get sidetracked with skirmishes and meaningless debates.

Instead, we keep our boxing gloves trained on what is eternal and lasting.

Heavenly Father, lead us away from silly fights. If we've fought and scrapped for all the wrong things, forgive us and let us start over.

PUSH OUT DEEPER: Luke 12:13–15; Exodus 2:14; Proverbs 26:20; Hebrews 13:5

Big Ol' Barns

"He said, 'I know what I'll do. I'll tear down my barns and build bigger ones so that I can store all my grain and goods in them.'"

LUKE 12:18 GW

THE DISCIPLES have no place to call home. Their purses are combined in common. They have no big ol' barns to fill with grain.

There's nothing wrong with having things.

It's when those things begin to own us that we lose our way.

The want of more things takes root, and it becomes greed. In pursuit of happiness, we stockpile, but it doesn't bring the happiness we thought it would. We nurture, we polish, we maintain. We build barns or rent storage units to house even more things—items we might not touch for years.

Our lives are cluttered with stuff, yet we want more.

Jesus didn't invest in things; he collected people. Dividends on those investments were—

> **Come With Me**
> *Is there a lasting impact from your investment?*

and continue to be—priceless. Our homes, our cars, our financial security belong to him. We don't store them, but use them to love people.

What does our treasure say about our lives?

PUSH OUT DEEPER: Luke 12:16–21; Revelation 3:17; Ecclesiastes 2:9–11; Matthew 6:21

Life Is More

> Then Jesus said to his disciples: "Therefore I tell you, do not worry
> about your life, what you will eat; or about your body, what you will
> wear. For life is more than food, and the body more than clothes."
>
> LUKE 12:22–23 NIV

SCRIPTURE NEVER REALLY tells us what the disciples look like. There are rare hints. We know James the son of Alphaeus is smaller in height, but only because it differentiates him from the other disciple named James. We know Peter is older than the others. Other than that, there are few details. We don't know what size shoe Jesus wears, or whether Simon Peter is stocky or thin.

Come With Me
Refine those things that write your story on the hearts of others.

While little in history describes what these followers wore or looked like, there are tomes written about their character.

Simon the Zealot is loyal. Bartholomew is respected. John is beloved by Jesus. Judas Iscariot struggles with greed.

Our character is our true identity, at least in hindsight. We are more than a body image or the clothes we wear. We are more than a few extra pounds around the waist. We are defined by how generously we love others. We are called his as we seek him every day.

Who we are is more than the superficial.

What is on the inside is what will be remembered.

PUSH OUT DEEPER: Luke 12:22–24; Proverbs 31:30; 1 Peter 3:4; Song of Solomon 4:7

Bags of Worry

"Can all your worries add a single moment to your life?"

LUKE 12:25 NLT

IF THE DISCIPLES were to stuff all of their worries in a bag and carry them around, how cumbersome would that be? They have plenty to worry about. The mood is changing, and powerful people scheme.

Jesus encourages the disciples to travel baggage-free in ministry, but also in life.

Worry is the fear of what *might* happen. It doesn't change the outcome. It doesn't help us plan. It offers no by-product other than misery. We take worry into our relationships and our conversations. It interrupts our sleep. It steals our contentment.

When tomorrow comes and that worrisome event didn't take place, we've been robbed. If it does, worry hasn't added a single virtue to handling the problem.

Consider the lilies. Jesus references these beautiful flowers, arrayed in colors of red, white, yellow, and purple. The lilies do not toil or spin in worry. They reach for the sunlight, and it's enough for today.

> ### Come With Me
> *What has worrying offered you other than misery? Enjoy today, and we'll work through the worry of tomorrow when it comes.*

Our worries will not add a single moment to our lives. Let's refuse to allow tomorrow's remote possibilities to steal today's good gifts.

PUSH OUT DEEPER: Luke 12:22–27; Matthew 6:33–34; Luke 10:41; Psalm 55:22

Seek First

> "But seek the kingdom of God, and all these things shall be added to you."
>
> LUKE 12:31 NKJV

TENSION RUNS HIGH. Men plot. It is natural for Jesus' disciples to wring their hands over the what-ifs. It's natural to want to hide. They don't know where they'll stay or rest their tired bodies. They're not certain of a next meal. They have real concerns, yet Jesus asks them to place their first thoughts on more eternal matters.

Seek *first* the kingdom of God.

For us as believers, faith is the center of who we are.

When we go to faith first, worry climbs down the ladder of importance.

> ### Come With Me
> Seek me first, before spiraling into worry. You'll find the faith you need.

We march into confidence as we are empowered with our most essential resources—trust, prayer, peace, direction—long before we allow worry to spin our thoughts.

New concerns will rise.

As we seek him first, worry will take its rightful place.

PUSH OUT DEEPER: Luke 12:28–31; Matthew 6:33; Romans 14:17; Psalm 143:8

Heavenly Deposit

> "Sell your material possessions, and give the money to the poor. Make yourselves wallets that don't wear out! Make a treasure for yourselves in heaven that never loses its value! In heaven thieves and moths can't get close enough to destroy your treasure."
>
> LUKE 12:33 GW

SILVER COINS support Jesus and his work. Those funds feed the poor and sustain ministry. Jesus never asks for money or attempts to build a religious empire. He spends everything they receive on the needs.

There is a heavenly depository that we'll never access on earth, but we are blessed as we make deposits. When we give sacrificially to further the gospel, that heavenly account prospers. When we use what we have to feed or educate or offer help to one who is in need, there's a boost in our account. What a blessing it is to give secretly, so that one hand doesn't know what the other is doing!

These deposits cannot be stolen.

One day we'll enter eternity and see the deposits, large and small, and how they multiplied in ways we never knew they could.

> **Come With Me**
> As you give, you discover the real meaning of treasure.

PUSH OUT DEEPER: Luke 12:31–33; Matthew 6:3; Ecclesiastes 5:10; Proverbs 22:9

Unfailing

"For where your treasure is, there your heart will be also."

LUKE 12:34 NIV

THE DISCIPLES LOVE receiving and giving good gifts, just like anyone else. Their bellies grumble at the smell of tantalizing food. They enjoy laughter and conversation as they recline around the table with friends.

The good days are really nice, but they also have tough days.

There are days when their faith is put on trial. Some days they make mistakes and feel terrible about it. There are days they deal with difficult people, and days they wake up uninspired.

> ### Come With Me
> *My love is unfailing and continual and never ends.*

Their circumstances are static, but because of their faith, they are secure.

Our faith holds strong when life is topsy-turvy and when things are smooth. Our security isn't tied to coffers of money or mountains of material goods. It's not tied to a good day or a bad day. It's tied to our treasure—God's constant, abundant love.

That treasure will never be found in things that come or go, but as we plant our roots in him. The vital issue is not the amount of our treasure but the location of it.

PUSH OUT DEEPER: Luke 12:32–34; Proverbs 4:23; Psalm 122:7; Proverbs 11:28

Be Ready

"Be dressed for service and keep your lamps burning, as though you were waiting for your master to return from the wedding feast. Then you will be ready to open the door and let him in the moment he arrives and knocks."

LUKE 12:35–36 NLT

A WEDDING IS A GRAND and solemn affair and goes on for days. Stewards watch over the household while a groom marries his bride. A steward oversees the servants and keeps the home ready, a fire roaring, and lights brightly lit. They do not know the exact hour that the master will arrive, but a good steward keeps the house ready as if he might come through the door at any time.

A poor steward acts as if the master will never return. In his absence, the household duties lapse. The dishes pile up. The servants are pushed around. The home falls into disarray.

In each case, the groom knocks on the door. One springs to open it, while the other rushes madly to put things into place.

Jesus is our groom, and he promises to return. We are to care for the church in his absence. We keep the fires burning as we fulfill his mission.

> ### Come With Me
> *Pray for my hardworking servants, and pray for my beloved church.*

We encourage his hardworking servants as they go about their duties.

His homecoming is imminent.

May we take care of the church, his beautiful bride.

PUSH OUT DEEPER: Luke 12:35–36; Revelation 3:20; Mark 2:20; 1 Thessalonians 4:16

Is This for Me?

Peter said, "Lord, are you telling this parable for us or for all?"

LUKE 12:41 ESV

THE DISCIPLES have proven they are ready to pack up and move to the next location and do whatever Jesus asks—no matter how rugged the undertaking. They are faithful servants. They will steward the church when the Master is away.

Jesus tells them a parable about two servants—one faithful, one bad. One keeps the home fires burning, always on the alert for his master's coming. The other plays when the master is away.

> ### Come With Me
> *Listening for my instructions is wise. Sometimes I'll give you the whole plan, but usually it's one part at a time.*

Peter is unsure of who Jesus is talking about. But he doesn't have to wonder what Jesus is thinking. He's close to Jesus and can approach without hesitation.

When we sense God speaking, we may not know what to do.

Are those words for me? Should I act on them? Lord, what do you want me to do?

We can ask our questions honestly. He's patient with us. We aren't expected to know all the details up front. He'll show us what he means. He'll say it as often as is needed until it soaks into our hearts. We'll learn along the way, and ask as many questions as we need.

PUSH OUT DEEPER: Luke 12:37–41; Hebrews 1:2; 1 John 2:27; John 14:26

Constrained

> "I came to cast fire on the earth, and would that it were already
> kindled! I have a baptism to be baptized with, and how great is
> my distress until it is accomplished!"
>
> LUKE 12:49–50 ESV

THE PHRASE "casting fire on the earth" sounds ominous, doesn't it?
The fire Jesus speaks about is the Holy Spirit, and it will kindle and
spread from the disciples to the multitude, to the uttermost parts of the
earth. Hear the urgency in Jesus' words. He will fulfill his mission, but
in order for the fire to spread, the church must rise to the challenge.

A final baptism will plunge Jesus into death,
and he'll ascend through murky waters in victory.
He longs for the church to ascend with him.

Don't constrain my work. Take care of my church.

These instructions are for the modern church.
The task is still great. If there are limitations, and
we are responsible, let's take them off. Let's remove
every restriction to reach the world with the gospel. Let's take the constraints off of prayer and believe in its power. Let's take the constraints
off the church and work together rather than divide.

> **Come With Me**
> *May my church rise as
> a thriving movement
> sweeping the nations.*

May we rise in response to his passionate cry. There are no limits to
what can be accomplished in his name when we remove the constraints.

Stir the embers, Jesus, in your church. Let the fire fall on us.

PUSH OUT DEEPER: Luke 12:42–50; 1 Corinthians 15:52;
John 5:28; 1 Thessalonians 4:17

Do You See?

> "You fools! You know how to interpret the weather signs of the earth and sky, but you don't know how to interpret the present times."
>
> LUKE 12:56 NLT

IF THE DISCIPLES CHOOSE JESUS, they choose conflict. Their faith will bring discord among family members who don't understand their choice. Their faith will be questioned and debated by people they love and respect.

Followers of Jesus will be singled out for persecution.

What are the signs? Do we see them?

When the sky is dark and clouds roll, we run for shelter. We grab our loved ones. We call friends to make sure they are taking shelter. If it's raining, we open our umbrellas and share.

The signs are all around us. Jesus said he would come back. As we notice the signs, let's share the good news with that loved one. Let's tell a friend about his love. Let us gather as many as we can and lead them to shelter.

Come With Me
I will return. That's my promise.

Jesus, your return isn't a fearful event. It's a glorious reunion. Just as you met face-to-face with the disciples, you long to meet face-to-face with us for eternity. We don't always know how to share this beautiful message, but give us the words. Move on the heart of that loved one or that friend who doesn't know you. Show us how to usher him or her into your love.

PUSH OUT DEEPER: Luke 12:51–59; John 14:3; Acts 1:11; Hebrews 9:28

Where Is Jesus?

Jesus replied to them, "Do you think that this happened to them
because they were more sinful than other people from Galilee?"

LUKE 13:2 GW

TWO TRAGEDIES have taken place within a short time: Pilate mur-
dered innocent men in the temple, and a tower collapsed in Siloam,
taking eighteen lives.

Is God a wrathful God?

Is tragedy punishment for sin?

Jesus sets them straight. Those who died at the hands of Pilate and
in the tower were cherished by God. Their deaths were not a result of
their sin. One was a tragic accident and the other the action of a cor-
rupt leader.

Where is Jesus in a tragedy? He's on the scene.
His comfort encircles a grieving heart. He offers
surpassing peace in a calamity. Our God is righ-
teously angry on our behalf when evil attempts
to triumph over good.

That leads to another important question:
Who are we in the heart of a tragedy?

We mourn with those who grieve. We stand against evil with those
harmed by evildoers. We close ranks with the suffering and serve as
his ambassadors.

> ### Come With Me
> *When tragedy strikes,
> close in around the
> suffering and let them
> know you care.*

PUSH OUT DEEPER: Luke 13:1–5; Joel 2:25; Joel 2:13; John 11:35

124

Another Chance

> "The gardener answered, 'Sir, give it one more chance. Leave it another year, and I'll give it special attention and plenty of fertilizer.'"
>
> LUKE 13:8 NLT

GRAPEVINES CURL AND CLIMB high in the vineyard, but one fails to thrive. The owner demands it be cut down, but the gardener intervenes.

There is hope for this vine.

The gardener sees its potential. Life is there, just waiting to sprout. It needs one more chance. One more year. One more fertilization. One more pruning season.

> **Come With Me**
>
> *While others desire to cut you down, I draw you closer to the Vine.*

While others may not see the growth waiting to explode inside of us, God does. Rather than compare us with others, he sees our potential.

He'll prune us. He'll water. He already envisions the fruit of love, joy, peace, gentleness, patience, faithfulness, goodness, and self-control developing in our lives.

When others want to give up on us, he is ready to see how tall we'll grow. Let's give ourselves, and others, another chance to become the fruitful vine we are destined to become.

PUSH OUT DEEPER: Luke 13:6–9; Ezekiel 17:8; John 15:1–2; Hosea 14:6–7

Celebrate

> When Jesus saw her, he called her forward and said to her, "Woman, you are set free from your infirmity." Then he put his hands on her, and immediately she straightened up and praised God.
>
> LUKE 13:12–13 NIV

SHE IS SO BENT OVER that all she sees is dirt and the soiled hems on people walking past. This condition has debilitated her body—and spirit—for eighteen long years.

She hears Jesus call her to him.

Is it possible he is speaking to her?

He puts his hands on her, and bones snap into place. She lifts her head and stands tall. She can't help but praise God!

It's the Sabbath, and a nearby official demands she end her celebration. He must be crazy. She's stared at the ground for eighteen years, and now she can see the sky!

No one can steal her joy.

> **Come With Me**
> Don't allow others to steal your gladness as you praise my name.

We are set free from our infirmities. Not everyone will understand it. Not everyone will believe it. If God has worked a miracle, let our praises ring!

PUSH OUT DEEPER: Luke 13:10–14; John 9:6–12; Psalm 33:9; Psalm 30:2

Work, Work, Work

"And ought not this woman, a daughter of Abraham whom Satan bound for eighteen years, be loosed from this bond on the Sabbath day?"

LUKE 13:16 ESV

MOSES STOOD ON THE MOUNT as God dictated the Ten Commandments. One commandment declared a Sabbath rest for God's people. God worked six days and rested on the seventh; the people were asked to rest too.

The Sabbath was not intended to be a legalistic rule that made God's people work, work, work, to earn the love of God.

Jesus points to the woman who has suffered way too long.

Ought not this woman, a daughter of Abraham, find rest too?

Ought not we find rest? A Sabbath rest quiets our minds. It offers respite for our bodies. A Sabbath rest provides balance in a world that keeps us in a whirlwind of activity. It's an invitation to slow down our busy pace to worship and refuel spiritually. A Sabbath rest is a gift for the soul, just as much as for the body.

> ### Come With Me
> *Give yourself permission to slow down, and let me give you the respite you so desperately need.*

PUSH OUT DEEPER: Luke 13:15–17; Deuteronomy 5:14; Hebrews 4:3; Matthew 11:28–29

Teeny-Tiny Faith

It is like a grain of mustard seed, which a man took, and cast into his garden; and it grew, and waxed a great tree; and the fowls of the air lodged in the branches of it.

LUKE 13:19 KJV

THE PROVERB OF THE MUSTARD SEED is a familiar one for the audience. A teeny-tiny mustard seed can grow several feet high. What if a seed of faith could grow in the same way?

God often asks us to do something big, and we feel really small. He asked the disciples to do this all the time. God worked through them in ways that made no sense—based on their background, on their temperament, and even on their age.

People are converted. People are healed. Some leap to their feet after years of begging on the street. Joy is restored to men and women who thought they'd never feel that way again.

The church is made up of believers who bring their teeny-tiny faith and plant it in good soil. That small grain takes root. It sprouts.

> **Come With Me**
>
> *My focus isn't on the size of your faith, but your faith in me. Bring your small seed of faith and watch what I can do with it.*

It flourishes like the mustard tree, which grows so large that birds roost in its mighty branches!

What will we do with our teeny-tiny faith?

We'll plant it, along with millions of others, and watch it grow.

PUSH OUT DEEPER: Luke 13:18–21; Mark 9:23; Jeremiah 32:17; Isaiah 40:26

Strait Gate

Strive to enter in at the strait gate: for many, I say unto you, will seek to enter in, and shall not be able.

LUKE 13:24 KJV

A STRAIT GATE IS TUCKED in a corner of the city. It's not the gate that leads to a broad highway outside the city, or the main gate where everyone gathers. The strait gate is off the beaten path. It winds up and down behind and around the city. Many take the strait gate to find their way to the back door of their home.

Come With Me

*Knock and I'll answer.
Let me show you
the way home.*

When a person knocks on the strait gate, it is opened immediately.

There is a strait gate that leads to heaven. When we knock, Jesus opens the door. This strait gate leads not to a broad path, but to the narrower paths of faith.

What waits behind the strait gate?

A life-changing road that leads away from the highway, as we walk with Jesus to find our way home.

PUSH OUT DEEPER: Luke 13:23–24; Matthew 7:13; Isaiah 35:8; Isaiah 30:21

One-to-One

> "Then you will say, 'But we ate and drank with you, and you taught in our streets.'"
>
> LUKE 13:26 NLT

HOW SAD TO IMAGINE eating and drinking and communing with Jesus, and yet he's a stranger. They know facts and outward details, but they don't know his heart. They are familiar with Jesus, but far from him.

Jesus drew a distinct line between knowing *about* him and knowing him. We are wise to pay attention to the difference. Faith can be tradition and rituals. It can be a place to go or a place to meet people. There's value in each of these, but knowing Jesus trumps them all.

> ### Come With Me
> Come sit with me, one-to-one, as a friend.

Knowing Jesus isn't a group activity. It begins one-to-one.

There's power in worshiping with believers. There's beauty in community. But if the crowd were to fall away, a one-to-one relationship still leads us to him. We aren't lonely without the crowd; we are alone with God.

Faith is not what we do, but an integral part of who we are.

PUSH OUT DEEPER: Luke 13:25–27; Hebrews 10:22; Psalm 119:151; Psalm 65:4

Grandfather Clause

"Indeed there are those who are last who will be first, and first who will be last."

LUKE 13:30 NIV

MANY OF THE EARLY FOLLOWERS have fallen away after time. They were curious about the most popular attraction in town, but their curiosity waned. Those who remain do so out of loyalty and love for Jesus. They believe in him and in his work.

In this culture, many of the religious believe their family name or a tie to the prophets is their ticket to heaven.

Jesus reminds anyone who desires to follow him that it is a personal invitation. They can stay. They can leave. Their lineage, however, won't take them to heaven. There is no grandfather clause in a relationship with God.

Our faith is individual.

It isn't earned by church attendance. It's not about a doctrine. It's not tied to a family tree.

Which of us would want that to be our connection, anyway?

> ### Come With Me
> I know every member of your family tree, but it's you I want to know.

It is our bond with Jesus that opens the door to faith and keeps it open until we enter eternity.

PUSH OUT DEEPER: Luke 13:28–30; Romans 5:18; Philippians 3:9; 1 Corinthians 1:30

Hearts to Repair

"Nevertheless, I must go on my way today and tomorrow and the day following, for it cannot be that a prophet should perish away from Jerusalem."

LUKE 13:33 ESV

HEROD'S POWER makes people tremble, but his threats don't trouble Jesus. Jesus' eyes are on sweet Jerusalem. It's his final destination on earth, from where he'll depart to his heavenly home. Herod's threats are hollow. They hold no power over Jesus. The only power that consumes him is to break the power of sin. Jesus will die at the hands of men like Herod so that grace might live.

Tell that fox I have work to do yet.

When our world is increasingly unfriendly to faith, those threats don't trouble us.

We set our hearts on work left undone. There are hearts to repair and eyes to be opened. We go on our way today and tomorrow and the day following, leaving criticism behind us as we listen to the Word instead.

> ## Come With Me
> *When your heart is firmly established in me and your eyes on those who are lost, critical words hold little power.*

Savior, please help us not to meet criticism with a critical spirit. There's so much to do, and we are so grateful to work alongside you. If we start to entangle ourselves in meaningless debates, speak softly and we'll move on.

PUSH OUT DEEPER: Luke 13:32–33; Colossians 1:23; Colossians 2:7–8; Jude 1:20–21

Under His Wing

"O Jerusalem, Jerusalem, the one who kills the prophets and stones those who are sent to her! How often I wanted to gather your children together, as a hen gathers her brood under her wings, but you were not willing!"

LUKE 13:34 NKJV

GOD SENT PROPHETS to wake the children of Israel from their rebellious behavior, but the prophets were killed and stoned.

The sorrow in Jesus' voice is unmistakable. God had so much more for his people, if only they had received him.

A temple is a glorious building, but without the presence of God, it's just stone and mortar. Religion, no matter how celebrated, is only form and function without the presence of the one whose name it bears.

There's so much more for us.

God longs to draw us near. He offers to protect and secure us like a chick under the wing of its mother. In our stubbornness, we often want to go our own way. We think we can do it without him. We can do many things on our own, but with the presence of God, we can do all things.

> ## Come With Me
> You can do many things on your own, but don't deny my tenderhearted voice gathering you close.

Gather us close, Jesus. Mark our churches with your presence. Complete our faith with your tender guidance. May we be so close that we hear your voice and our lives are marked with your power. Gather us under your wing.

PUSH OUT DEEPER: Luke 13:34–35; Psalm 91:4; Ruth 2:12; Psalm 63:7

Watched

On a day of worship Jesus went to eat at the home of a prominent
Pharisee. The guests were watching Jesus very closely.

LUKE 14:1 GW

THE MEAL IS DELICIOUS. It's a feast! Jesus is watched closely as
he eats. The Pharisees hope to trick him, but Jesus isn't concerned
about their devious plans or their close observance.

Whether he is in a friendly room or the home of a trickster, Jesus
remains true to his nature.

Our lives can reflect Jesus, or they can confuse others about Jesus. We
are continually observed, even when we don't realize it. Our words on
social media are viewed by those we don't know well. Our everyday activi-
ties are scrutinized by eyes we don't see looking.

We don't want to live as if we are in a bubble.
We don't want to pretend. Yet we are wise to realize that a world watches closely to see if this Jesus
we claim is worth following.

Father, may those who watch see the richness
of our relationship with you. May they see the
reach of mercy and what it looks like to start over when we've made
mistakes. Our greatest desire is to remain true to our identity as a child
of God, whether eyes are watching or not.

> **Come With Me**
> *If you've messed up,
> take responsibility
> and start anew.*

PUSH OUT DEEPER: Luke 14:1–2; Ephesians 6:6; Galatians 1:10; 1 Thessalonians 2:4

Burden Lifted

And they had nothing to say.

LUKE 14:6 NIV

THE MAN'S BODY is painfully swollen. His arms and lower extremities are enlarged. The miracle worker is at a nearby table.

Will there be a miracle today? Will that miracle be his?

The religious leaders have positioned the afflicted man in front of Jesus. He is part of the setup. Healing on the Sabbath has been a point of contention between the Pharisees and Jesus from the beginning, and this is a test.

Jesus takes the man's hands in his own. As he prays, the distorted and pain-filled limbs shrink to normal. Pain leaves.

The Pharisees are quietly celebrating, but not over the man's healing. They've just piled one more accusation against Jesus.

> **Come With Me**
> *Don't turn away from your obvious need in shame; turn toward me.*

Two distinct burdens could have been healed that day. One is the obvious physical burden plaguing the man. The other is a handicap the Pharisees willingly placed on their own hearts.

It's easy to point out someone else's need, but what about our own?

We can ask the Great Physician to examine us. He points out that unhealthy root of rejection. He maps out those damaged areas of our hearts. He shows us thoughts that lead us away from God's best.

His report is never one of condemnation, but a prescription for what ails us and a plan of action.

PUSH OUT DEEPER: Luke 14:2–6; Matthew 11:30; Matthew 23:4; 1 John 5:3

Humility or Humiliation

"For those who exalt themselves will be humbled, and those who
humble themselves will be exalted."

LUKE 14:11 NLT

SEVERAL TABLES are clustered in the room. The center seat at each
is an honorary seat. Jesus watches as men eye those prized seats.
Some take the chief positions, while others take lesser seats.

Once everyone is seated, Jesus tells a story.

A man chooses a seat of honor at a wedding. When a more noble
person walks through the door, the host has no other option but to re-
assign the first man to a different seat. If the man
had chosen a lesser seat from the beginning, he'd
have been spared the humiliation.

What a lesson in humility!

Humility is a better position than potential
humiliation, for certain. Yet this isn't about getting
a better seat. Jesus reminds us to consider others
as greater. True humility is unpretentious and unassuming. It doesn't
seek the lion's share of the limelight, but loves to shed a light on others.

When we are considerate, we don't need the best seat in the house.
Our greatest affirmation comes from above.

> **Come With Me**
> *In a world where people
> strive to be noticed,
> let humility lead.*

PUSH OUT DEEPER: Luke 14:7–11; Proverbs 15:33; James 4:10; Proverbs 29:23

Hospitality

"But when you give a feast, invite the poor, the crippled, the lame,
the blind, and you will be blessed, because they cannot repay you.
For you will be repaid at the resurrection of the just."

LUKE 14:13–14 ESV

I F AN INVITATION IS GIVEN, one is expected in return.

If a gift is given on a special day, surely it will be reciprocated.

If a neighbor is loaned a loaf of bread, that neighbor will receive a loaf of bread when he knocks on the door in need.

But the lame, the crippled, the blind? They can't repay an invitation, for they have no home. They can't return a gift, because they don't have it to give. If they have a loaf of bread, it may be the only meal they have to offer their own family.

Come With Me

Show generous hospitality to one who cannot possibly return your gift.

The feast Jesus describes is an act of generosity. The host brings in the lost, the lame, the blind and gives them the best he has to offer. He doesn't expect the favor to be returned. It's a no-holds-barred act of kindness.

Generosity isn't an act; it is an attitude. When we give without expecting anything in return, we become an instrument of blessing, but we are also blessed as a result. We are released from the need to be paid back, and our attitude and acts become true generosity.

PUSH OUT DEEPER: Luke 14:12–14; Proverbs 22:9; Proverbs 19:17; Matthew 10:42

Invited

"But they all alike began to make excuses. The first said, 'I have just bought a field, and I must go and see it. Please excuse me.'"

LUKE 14:18 NIV

A SERVANT IS SENT to tell the invited that the meal is ready. When the servant returns, no guests are with him. Only a fistful of excuses. One man needs to see a field. Another just bought oxen and needs to try them out. The last guest is newly married, and this isn't a good time to come.

The host sees through all of these excuses.

The first man could have looked at his field another day.

The second could have tried out the oxen at a later hour.

The newly married man could have brought his bride to the feast.

Come With Me

Come sit at the table with me. Bring those you love. There is a seat waiting for them as well.

We are invited to dine with Christ. That invitation is extended with grace. It's a feast set before us, filled with spiritual blessings that reach to the heavens. Nothing is more valuable than the gift Jesus offers so readily.

What is our excuse? Our busy lives aren't greater than his presence. Our desires pale in comparison to his purpose. Our relationships are important, but not greater than loving Jesus.

Let's yield to his extravagant invitation.

PUSH OUT DEEPER: Luke 14:16–20; Isaiah 55:1; Revelation 21:6; John 4:10

Just As We Are

"And the master said to the servant, 'Go out to the highways and hedges and compel people to come in, that my house may be filled.'"

LUKE 14:23 ESV

SERVANTS RUN DOWN highways and byways. They search under hedges for vagrants. They compel everyone they meet to come to the city to dine at their master's home.

An unlikely crowd gathers. One limps. Another holds on to the shoulder of the sighted person in front of him. One brushes the dust from his filthy robes.

When they arrive, a servant washes their feet. Another servant takes them to a table, laden with food like they've not eaten before.

Is it possible all of this is for them?

It *is* possible, and a feast awaits us as well. We'll enter the gates of heaven. Jesus will greet us. We'll be seated at the table next to others forgiven of their sins. Heaven will be filled with an unlikely crowd—and we are among that number.

> **Come With Me**
> *My house has many rooms. I want to fill them all.*

Jesus compels us to come dine with him today and every day. He asks that we come, and also compels us to go out to the highways and byways to spread the invitation.

Let's tell the world: Come to the Master's house—just as you are.

PUSH OUT DEEPER: Luke 14:21–24; Revelation 3:20; John 21:12; Acts 28:28

My Disciple

> "But don't begin until you count the cost. For who would begin
> construction of a building without first calculating the cost to see
> if there is enough money to finish it?"
>
> LUKE 14:28 NLT

JESUS' VIEWS are unlike anyone else's. His works are incomparable. It's exciting to think about joining the team! Jesus is blunt with those who want to be a part.

There is a cost to kingdom building.

Following Jesus is a cross-bearing venture with a definitive purpose.

If we want to be his disciples, we are called to love him over anything else.

We are asked to carry our own cross. Only the Son of God can carry the sins of the world, but we *will* bear a cross as we follow Jesus and sympathize with the broken, as we pray for the lost, and as we live our faith in a world that doesn't always accept it.

Come With Me
Following me isn't always a charmed life, but it is a changed life.

Following Jesus is revolutionary faith. There is a cost, and sometimes that cost is great. No matter how much we give, however, it's pennies on the dollar compared to the spiritual inheritance we receive in return.

PUSH OUT DEEPER: Luke 14:25–28; 1 Peter 5:1; Romans 8:18; 2 Corinthians 4:17

Overcomer

> "Or suppose a king is going to war against another king. He would
> first sit down and think things through. Can he and his 10,000
> soldiers fight against a king with 20,000 soldiers?"
>
> LUKE 14:31 GW

KINGS GO TO BATTLE. Lives, land, and titles are won and lost.
It's a fact of life.

But no king impetuously wages war.

First he scrutinizes his enemy. He won't go to war against the unknown. He and his generals will learn everything they can about him.
He'll learn about his weaknesses, his strengths, his tactics.

> **Come With Me**
> *You are an overcomer,
> for I have equipped
> you for battle.*

He examines his own resources. The king
numbers the troops. He considers his arsenal and
the readiness of his army. He checks the storehouse for food and water. Barricades are tested
and weapons are readied. Once he's done all of
this, the king is ready for battle.

We too face a real enemy. We learn about the
enemy's tactics so that we can defeat him on God's turf. We gird up for
spiritual war in our thoughts and hearts. We reach for weapons that have
divine power to demolish strongholds. We wage battle against the enemy
who desires to distract us from God's best, but we have counted the cost.

We've girded up spiritually, for we are equipped with everything we
need to overcome, if only we'll use it.

PUSH OUT DEEPER: Luke 14:29–32; Hebrews 11:30; Joshua 23:10; Colossians 2:15

Hello

"So therefore, any one of you who does not renounce all that he has cannot be my disciple."

LUKE 14:33 ESV

THE DISCIPLES are familiar with saying good-bye.

Peter, Andrew, James, and John said good-bye to their fishing enterprise. Matthew said good-bye to authority and power. All of the disciples said good-bye to family members and familiarity. With each good-bye, they said hello to something new.

Their good-byes rang bittersweet, but their hellos led them in a new direction.

When the Holy Spirit says it's time to leave, we might look backward. We want to say good-bye to all those things we love.

What if we look at the hello waiting for us?

We'll anticipate the new, rather than mourning the old.

> **Come With Me**
> Be open to my new assignment for you. Saying good-bye is sad for a moment, but there's something beautiful for you ahead.

We'll stop looking in the rearview mirror at what we left behind and see the adventure ahead. We are human. We'll always value what we leave behind, but if we cling to it, we may miss the new season God has for us.

Let's say hello to the fresh season ahead.

PUSH OUT DEEPER: Luke 14:33; Philippians 3:7; Philippians 1:21; Romans 14:8

Salty

> "Salt is good, but if it loses its saltiness, how can it be made salty again? It is fit neither for the soil nor for the manure pile; it is thrown out. Whoever has ears to hear, let them hear."
>
> LUKE 14:34–35 NIV

LIGHT AND SALT are distinctive by what they offer to objects lacking those properties. A dark room is illuminated by a light. A ship lost in a storm is drawn to shore by the beacon. A lackluster meal is seasoned perfectly with the right amount of salt!

Unless the light is dim. Unless the beacon fades and goes out. Unless the salt has lost its tang.

The Pharisees have access to the salt and light Jesus offers, but they are flickering bulbs in the vast darkness. They pour out words over the hearts of others, but their messages offer little value. They shine glaring lights of condemnation that burn up rather than heal their audience.

> **Come With Me**
>
> *Generously pour salt and light over the world around you.*

What a compelling wake-up call for those of us who call ourselves believers.

Jesus calls us to a salty life, not one that blends in. May we live so salty that it pours generously over our home and those who abide within its walls. May it bring savor and restorative properties to our relationships.

May those who don't know Jesus walk away with a hunger to know him better, having experienced the salt and light in our words and actions.

PUSH OUT DEEPER: Luke 14:34–35; John 6:40; John 9:5; Philippians 2:15

Grumblers

And the Pharisees and the scribes grumbled, saying, "This man receives sinners and eats with them."

LUKE 15:2 ESV

THERE ARE LOTS OF WORDS that describe grumbling.

Bellyaching. Complaining. Protesting. Griping. Whining.

Grumbling leaves a mark. It's damaging in almost any relationship. If the religious crowd would listen to Jesus rather than murmur and complain, they might hear what he's trying to teach them. His promises are just as much for them as they are for others.

If they cease their grumbling, their story may take a drastic turn. But they don't.

Grumble, grumble, grumble.

How does our bellyaching rewrite the stories in our own lives? When our immediate reaction to a person or situation is a complaint, it leaves little room for transformation. If we walk around with our defenses hackled, there's little room for resolution.

> ### Come With Me
> *Give that habit to me with a willing heart. Get ready for contentment to take its place.*

If grumbling is our natural response, let's pause our complaints long enough to listen to the Holy Spirit. Let's ask him to redirect our natural inclination of *grumble, grumble, grumble* with supernatural help.

Grumbling is a habit; it's not a descriptor of who we really are.

PUSH OUT DEEPER: Luke 15:1–2; Exodus 16:7; Philippians 2:14; John 6:43

In Search of a Shepherd

"Suppose one of you has a hundred sheep and loses one of them.
Doesn't he leave the ninety-nine in the open country and go after
the lost sheep until he finds it?"

LUKE 15:4 NIV

A SHEPHERD CHECKS THE FENCES. He walks at night with a lighted flame, ensuring his herd is bedded down for the night and predators are at bay. When he wakens, one is missing. He leaves the ninety-nine in the care of his assistant shepherd and strikes out across the open country. He won't come back until the lamb is draped across his broad shoulders.

This story isn't just about a lost sheep.

It's the joy of seeing a shepherd come over the rise. That sheep has sought a way out of the ravines and thickets. It longs for nothing more than green pastures and a cool drink of water. When the sheep sees the shepherd at a distance, it rejoices.

It is no longer adrift. Home isn't far away.

We were once lost, but now we are found!

May we never forget the joy of a shepherd's rescue. He sought us. He traversed across the heavens and trampled over sin, going into the deepest ravines, safely carrying us home in his nail-scarred hands.

> ## Come With Me
>
> *If you feel far from home, look up. I'm there. You are found!*

PUSH OUT DEEPER: Luke 15:3–6; 1 Timothy 1:15; Luke 19:10; Ezekiel 34:11–13

Rejoice!

"I tell you that in the same way there will be more rejoicing in heaven over one sinner who repents than over ninety-nine righteous persons who do not need to repent."

LUKE 15:7 NIV

GENERATIONS EARLIER in a lush garden, evil tiptoed in and robbed God. The deceiver traipsed before heaven with his prize held high, believing himself to be greater than his Creator.

That's why a celestial party erupts for every lost sheep that returns home safe and sound.

Every redeemed sinner is worthy of joy.

Jesus broke open the tomb, and humanity is no longer held captive. There is no lie persuasive enough, no chain thick enough, no pit deep enough to keep the repentant and the lost from running into the arms of redemption.

> **Come With Me**
> *You have loved me willingly, and that brings me great pleasure.*

Our heavenly Father rejoices over all who love him with their soul, spirit, and being.

We join in this holy celebration.

We cheer in gratitude for our own salvation, but we also applaud every single soul rescued by his love.

PUSH OUT DEEPER: Luke 15:7; Matthew 10:32; Genesis 15:6; Psalm 101:6

Adrift

"Or suppose a woman has ten silver coins and loses one. Doesn't she light a lamp, sweep the house and search carefully until she finds it?"

LUKE 15:8 NIV

WHEN THE WOMAN REALIZES the silver coin is lost, she doesn't go outside to look. Instead, she lights a lamp and kneels, searching every nook and hiding place within the home.

She sweeps the dirt floors, hoping it will come into the light. When she sees a glint of silver, she rejoices! She collects it carefully and puts it with the other nine.

It's safe! It's hers. It's back where it belongs. In the parable of the lost sheep, a sheep stumbled *out* of the fold and the shepherd searched until it was found. Here, a coin is lost *in* the house.

It's possible to be in the house of God and to be adrift.

> **Come With Me**
> *I'm drawing you back to vibrant faith within my church.*

Just as Jesus represents the shepherd, the woman represents the Holy Spirit, who sweeps every inch of the house until the silver coin, marked by the king, is nestled safely with the other coins.

We are marked with the image of a King.

He sees when we are wandering and disconnected, even in the heart of the church. He searches for us and does not stop until our heart is safely back where it belongs.

PUSH OUT DEEPER: Luke 15:8–10; John 6:39–40; Jeremiah 31:14; Psalm 51:12

Far From Home

"After a few days, the younger son gathered his possessions and left for a country far away from home. There he wasted everything he had on a wild lifestyle."

LUKE 15:12 GW

A SON REBELS. He gathers his belongings and leaves home. Within a short time, he squanders his inheritance, spending not just his money but his well-being.

Jesus introduces his listeners to the Father.

He paints a clear picture of a daddy mourning when one of his children is far from home. The son doesn't realize he's stepped into destruction, because it feels good in the moment. The son doesn't realize his inheritance is slipping away, for he's immune to consequences as long as one more coin lingers in the bag.

But the Father knows.

> **Come With Me**
> *That prodigal on your heart is also on mine.*

He sees the pigsty just ahead. He is mindful of loneliness and shame that will arise on a bleak day. Our heavenly Father is keenly aware when we ramble down a road of sin, away from his arms. He sees the trap of one who desires to steal away our inheritance.

He's waiting with open arms for us to come home.

PUSH OUT DEEPER: Luke 15:10–13; Ezekiel 34:12; 1 Timothy 1:15; Matthew 18:11

Famine

"After he had spent everything, there was a severe famine in that whole country, and he began to be in need."

LUKE 15:14 NIV

HOW DID THE PRODIGAL SON'S inheritance disappear so quickly? It was enough to last a lifetime!

Where are those friends who gathered around as drink flowed and the party rumbled? They said they were true friends, but now they are nowhere to be seen.

The son, who once had everything, is left with nothing of value. He can't find a job because of the famine. He tries to find hope, but his new-found state of being is bleak. He looks longingly back at what he once thought trivial. All he has left is a fistful of regrets.

> **Come With Me**
>
> *That thing you want so much—it will never make you happy. Contentment is where you'll find joy.*

The things we take for granted are the things we miss the most when they are gone. Material goods dim in comparison to the relationships we ignore in the pursuit. Reckless living seems foolish when we measure all we lost in the chase.

What are we investing in? Are they lasting? Do they offer long-term benefits over immediate satisfaction?

Savior, thank you for all you've given us. It's enough, it's a gift! We don't need something else or something bigger. We don't want our life to look like anyone else's. Help us to invest in where we are—right now, today!

PUSH OUT DEEPER: Luke 15:14–15; Psalm 34:10; Psalm 103:5; Psalm 90:14

Waiting Arms

> "So he returned home to his father. And while he was still a long
> way off, his father saw him coming. Filled with love and compas-
> sion, he ran to his son, embraced him, and kissed him."
>
> LUKE 15:20 NLT

NO JEWISH MAN GATHERS his robes and runs. It is undignified.
It's unheard of! Yet that's exactly what this father does when he
sees his son trudging up the road. He grabs his boy with both arms,
embraces him, and kisses him soundly.

Undignified, yes. Joy-filled, absolutely!

It's the opposite of what the son expected. When he sees his father
running down the road, he braces, for he took his father's greatest gift
and wasted it on wild living. The rank odor of the pigsty where he took
his meals lingers in the folds of his garment. He is
gaunt and hungry, far from the healthy boy who
left home.

In his embrace, a father's forgiveness is greater
than his many sins.

When everyone else has given up on us, including ourselves, we are not without hope. Our
Abba Father sees beyond outward appearances to a remorseful heart.
The weight of the world may be all others can see, but a repentant spirit
will not be turned away. We aren't imprisoned by our mistakes. We are
empowered as we take the road back to a Father's waiting arms.

> **Come With Me**
> *My delight is
> unrestrained when one
> of my own returns.*

PUSH OUT DEEPER: Luke 15:16–20; 2 Samuel 14:33; Genesis 46:29; John 21:16

The Best Robe

But the father said to his servants, Bring forth the best robe, and
put it on him; and put a ring on his hand, and shoes on his feet.

LUKE 15:22 KJV

SERVANTS STAND AGAPE. Could this be the son of their master?
Wine stains splotch the man's garment. A stench reaches their
noses with unflinching boldness. The man in the master's embrace is
travel weary and thin. He doesn't resemble the arrogant young man
who left months earlier.

Their master calls out. *Grab the best robe, please. Put a ring on his
finger. And don't forget the shoes.*

They gather the items. They peel away foul clothing. One servant
slips the family ring on his finger while another bends to slip shoes on
his foul feet. Once the son is wrapped in the best
robe, the message is clear.

The master has made his claim.

Once upon a time, sin cloaked humanity, dark
and destructive. Jesus challenged the deceiver,
who dared to steal away his children. That sacrifice clothed and covered our sinful state, and his
broken body claimed us as sons and daughters.

> ### Come With Me
> *Take my best robe, that
> of my redeeming love,
> and let it cover you.*

He offers the best robe, that of righteousness. He bathes us in new
life and offers food for our souls. We are safe. We are his.

PUSH OUT DEEPER: Luke 15:21–24; Acts 1:24; 1 Samuel 16:7; 1 John 2:12

What About Me?

"His older son was in the field. As he was coming back to the house, he heard music and dancing."

LUKE 15:25 GW

THE OLDER SON STANDS in waist-high crops that are flourishing under his care. Sounds of music and celebration filter from the main house. He questions a field hand, asking why the music is so loud in the middle of the day. He stiffens at the unforeseen answer.

Your brother's home.

News travels fast in such a small region. His brother's actions have insulted this family's honor. The harder one brother works to embarrass the family, the more the other brother tries to do what is right.

Jealousy. Hurt. Anger. They're what he feels. It's not fair.

Yet his father's joy over his returned son doesn't diminish his joy over a son who has remained faithful. Surely the angels celebrate the homecoming of every sinner, and we are just as privileged to cheer each prodigal who finds their way back into the arms of the Master. While we do so, let us not underestimate the pleasure that faithfulness produces in the heart of our Father. Just as he runs toward the prodigal, he seeks to find the faithful. He rejoices over every child who calls him Abba Father.

> ### Come With Me
> *Just as I am faithful to you, your faithfulness gladdens the heavens.*

PUSH OUT DEEPER: Luke 15:25–32; Genesis 15:6; Matthew 25:21; 2 Chronicles 16:9a

Shrewd

"The rich man had to admire the dishonest rascal for being so shrewd. And it is true that the children of this world are more shrewd in dealing with the world around them than are the children of the light."

LUKE 16:8 NLT

THE PHARISEES AND SCRIBES are near enough to hear, but his words aren't for them. He pulls the disciples close. Though the religious men claim to take a moral high road, Jesus reveals their hidden motivation: money.

He describes a rogue who steals from his master and is caught. The servant swiftly goes to his master's account holders, one by one. He cuts one debt in half, another by 20 percent. When he loses his job, these satisfied debtors may take him in.

Is it possible Jesus is commending this thief's actions? No, Jesus is contrasting one method with another. The thief dishonestly used his master's money for his own safety and purposes. The disciples have been given open access to the Master's resources to build his church. They will need to be shrewd, but with their motivation planted in good soil. Their investments will have eternal rewards, both for them and for the recipients.

Everything we own is for a greater purpose. Everything we touch leaves a legacy. We are called to be wise. Our eyes always on the prize of eternity, and safety for those who do not yet know Jesus. That is the richest reward of all.

Come With Me

I multiply every sacrifice made on the behalf of the kingdom, in ways you cannot imagine.

PUSH OUT DEEPER: Luke 16:1–9; Psalm 112:5; 2 Corinthians 9:12–13; Proverbs 3:9

Dividend

"One who is faithful in a very little is also faithful in much, and one who is dishonest in a very little is also dishonest in much."

LUKE 16:10 ESV

MONEY HOLDS LITTLE SIGNIFICANCE for the Son of God. His concerns are not with coins clanking in a bag, but for the spirits of the men who listen to his words.

Peter. Simon the Zealot. John the Beloved. James the son of Alphaeus. All of these men are closely aligned in friendship with Jesus. He generously teaches them to be faithful in what is considered *much*—not necessarily in the world, but in the framing of a faithful life. If they are faithful in their private thoughts, in their love for God, in their hunger for righteousness, that can't help but spill out into everyday acts of faithfulness.

> **Come With Me**
> *The world may see faithfulness as a small thing, but I applaud as you choose integrity and intimacy with me.*

This parallel is just as encouraging for us as it was for his disciples.

Surely we desire to live with integrity in everyday details. Yet where do we place our greatest investment? As we devote ourselves to those things considered *much* in the kingdom of God, we reap the dividends. We invest as we read his Word, as we make one right choice when no one is looking. We invest in one-on-one time with our heavenly Father. As we do so, integrity in the small stuff tumbles from the overflow of such a beautiful investment.

PUSH OUT DEEPER: Luke 16:10–12; Proverbs 27:19; James 1:22; Romans 2:13

Master, Master

"A servant cannot serve two masters. He will hate the first master and love the second, or he will be devoted to the first and despise the second. You cannot serve God and wealth."

LUKE 16:13 GW

MANY SERVANTS ARE BROUGHT into a household to serve out a debt. Others are born into servanthood. Each attends the master and his family's needs from morning to evening. Freedom often seems elusive, yet it is a daily wish.

No person willingly walks into slavery, yet the love of money can be a demanding master. It compels us to slave away the days of our youth, and we may miss the most precious of gifts. It demands we own the latest or best, when in reality those debts have the power to own us.

> ### Come With Me
> Love me first. Love me wholly. Your greatest needs are not fulfilled by a pursuit of more, but in your relationship with me.

Money by itself is a means of blessing, but the love of money requires a higher and higher price tag.

Will we serve money, or will it be of service to others?

Will we serve money, or will we release it liberally as our Lord leads?

When our allegiance is to our Savior, he becomes our sole master—the only one whose intention is to set us totally free.

PUSH OUT DEEPER: Luke 16:13–14; Isaiah 33:6; Matthew 6:19; 1 Timothy 6:10

Hollow Hearts

The Pharisees, who dearly loved their money, heard all this and scoffed at him.

Luke 16:14 nlt

ONE TUGS AT HIS BEARD and shakes his head. Another ridicules Jesus openly. The Pharisees dearly love their money, and the story Jesus has told points a finger at their greed. They point back, jeering at Jesus' obvious poverty. He has no home. His feet are dusty. He and his disciples live like peasants, for they hold no possessions—except for what they have in common, and even those they give away.

If money and possessions are the cusp of life, then the scoffers must have it all. They must know it all. Yet Jesus stresses that when our hearts are barren, we have nothing of value. A greedy heart is unfertile. Possessions and a love of money will never fill the hollow place created by such a lack.

What do these men miss as they resist Jesus' wise words?

What do we miss when we resist the leading of the Holy Spirit?

Rather than resist, what if we soak in every word and let his wisdom drench our hollow places? As we listen to and obey the Holy Spirit—especially in those areas where we cling way too tight—he leads us from hollow places to hallowed ground.

> ## Come With Me
> Will you heed my instruction? My intention isn't to take away anything from you, but to give you what you so desperately need.

PUSH OUT DEEPER: Luke 16:14–15; Ecclesiastes 4:13; Proverbs 8:33; Proverbs 4:1

Spirit of the Law

"It is easier for the earth and the heavens to disappear than to drop a comma from the Scriptures."

LUKE 16:17 GW

GENERATIONS EARLIER, Moses climbed a mountain to be alone with God. He returned with the words of God etched on a stone tablet. He raced to tell the Israelites what God had spoken, declaring the spirit of the law—a plan designed to bring God's children close and to break the stronghold of sin.

Now in Jesus' time, many of the religious outwardly follow the rule of the law, but they have forgotten the spirit of the law. God desired to live in relationship with his children. He steered his people from covetousness to community. From idol worship to one-to-one connection with the one true God. Every comma and stroke of the law was designed to draw his people near.

> ### Come With Me
> *If you've been trying to love me by following rules, come sit with me. Let me show you a different way.*

When Jesus died on the cross, he fulfilled the law. His sacrifice transitioned God's people from rules to engaging in relationship with our heavenly Father. When we embrace friendship with God, rules are no longer our emphasis.

We obey him because we *love* him. We seek him because we *know* him.

Every word spoken generations earlier to Moses thrives as the spirit of the law lives within the hearts of God's people.

PUSH OUT DEEPER: Luke 16:16–17; Exodus 34:28; Hebrews 10:16; 1 Corinthians 11:25

Hold Her Close

"Everyone who divorces his wife and marries another commits adultery, and he who marries a woman divorced from her husband commits adultery."

LUKE 16:18 ESV

WHY IS JESUS SUDDENLY talking about divorce? It feels out of context in the conversation, but all along he's been talking about treasure. This is not a deviation, but an addendum.

Women are often overlooked in this culture. The men in the room are community leaders, and many follow their lead. A trend has developed as men divorce their wives—for as little reason as a meal prepared to less than satisfaction. In this warning, Jesus admonishes these spiritual leaders to treasure their wives.

Jesus broke tradition, especially when it came to women. He taught them, just as he did the men. He crossed the street to talk to women caught in sin in order to liberate them. He invited women to support his ministry. All of these were cultural groundbreakers. Divorce left a woman unprotected and damaged her reputation. He declared these women were worthy of safekeeping.

> **Come With Me**
> *I am your shelter,*
> *your rock, and*
> *your safeguard.*

He declares we are worthy as well. He is our protector. He values each of us. His truth is greater than cultural perceptions, and his love is our greatest shield.

PUSH OUT DEEPER: Luke 16:18; Matthew 27:55; John 19:25; John 4:26–29

Crossings

"The time came when the beggar died and the angels carried him to Abraham's side. The rich man also died and was buried."

LUKE 16:22 NIV

A RICH MAN LIVES in a fine house. He wears clothes made of purple linen. His lifestyle is flamboyant, from his clothing to his sumptuous meals to his property. Even the gate to his house is luxurious, lovely to the eye, except for the sore-covered man starving at its base.

What disparity between these two! One hopes for crumbs to fall from the other's table. One lives for his own pleasure, blind to the needs just outside his door. The disparity between them remains just as wide when they die. A majestic angel carries the sore-covered, weary, starving man to heaven. His body is healed. His hunger abated.

The other walks into an eternity of suffering.

This story, recounted by Jesus, doesn't condemn wealth, but rather leads us to examine what we do with it and how we define it. There are riches found in our relationship with our heavenly Father. There are riches in noticing that one who is downtrodden and just outside the door.

Our time on earth often seems measureless. It's but a brief crossing from this life to eternity. When we love God and love others in our short time on earth, we accrue riches that can never be diminished.

Come With Me

Let all your days reflect the faith that resides in your heart.

PUSH OUT DEEPER: Luke 16:19–22; Psalm 90:12; Matthew 6:19–20; 1 John 2:17

Send a Message

> "Then he said, 'I beg you therefore, father, that you would send him to my father's house, for I have five brothers, that he may testify to them, lest they also come to this place of torment.'"
>
> LUKE 16:27–28 NKJV

IN HIS EARTHLY LIFE, the rich man had far-reaching influence. All he had to do was to send a message, and most heeded his call. *Bring me this. Do that for me. Take care of my need.*

Perhaps for the first time, he looks beyond his own wishes to those of his family. He bids someone to tell them the importance of a godly life while there is still time. He asks that they be spared the torment he discovered too late.

His request is denied, but not due to a lack of compassion. He has heard the message. It has been shouted for generations. The prophets and Moses rang out warnings, calling God's people to relationship with him. Jesus himself walks the earth, sent by God to rescue his people.

We will send thousands of messages to loved ones—texts, calls, talking in person, perhaps even an old-fashioned letter.

In all of these messages, do we tell those we love about Jesus?

Do we bid them come closer, while there is yet time?

Let's send a message to those we love the most, introducing them to a heavenly Father who has been reaching for them their entire lives.

Come With Me

Tell that one that I have loved them always. Don't shy away from sharing such good news.

PUSH OUT DEEPER: Luke 16:23–31; Mark 16:15; Jeremiah 25:5; Matthew 24:14

Little Ones

One day Jesus said to his disciples, "There will always be temptations
to sin, but what sorrow awaits the person who does the tempting!"

LUKE 17:1 NLT

JESUS OFTEN REFERRED to children as "little ones." On this day, he is
talking about the new believers who have given so much to follow him.
These new believers don't always know what to do and don't have all the
answers, but they step out of their normal routines to walk in greater faith.

In this conversation, we cannot help but hear
Jesus' protective nature over these "little ones."

> **Come With Me**
>
> *It's easy to forget how
> far I've brought you
> and the miracles I've
> performed in your life.
> Let's celebrate that
> again, together. Then
> tell someone who needs
> to hear it today.*

May we be just as caring over those who are
new to faith. Let's not forget we had questions in
the beginning. May we remember how hard it was
to discern right from wrong, or how to discern
the voice of the Holy Spirit over our own desires.

We may never intend to lead others into sin.
Yet our attitude or words of judgment may tempt
them toward discouragement. Let's show them
the way with patience. Let's pray for that one who
is a work in progress. When we see that "little one" battling temptation,
let's recall the times we stumbled and what we learned through our
mistakes. Let's cheer them on! Let's celebrate how faithful God is to
complete the work he began in all of us.

PUSH OUT DEEPER: Luke 17:1–2; Psalm 36:5; Hebrews 10:25; 1 Thessalonians 5:11

We Are Free

> "Pay attention to yourselves! If your brother sins, rebuke him, and if he repents, forgive him."
>
> LUKE 17:3 ESV

JESUS ASKS AN INTERESTING QUESTION. How do we respond to the person who puts a stumbling block in our path?

Our flesh is affronted. It hurts when someone tosses a stumbling block in our path with their words, attitude, or actions. We are angry. We're wounded. We're silent. We may even put a polite smile on our face, but we build the walls high. They can come close but are not allowed in.

One stumbling block leads to another.

Is there another way?

We are free to speak the truth, in love.

We are free to work through conflict.

We are encouraged to mend broken places in a relationship, if possible.

If that person chooses not to work through the issue, we aren't stuck in a cycle of payback. If she does say she is sorry, we are free to forgive and start the relationship anew.

> ## Come With Me
>
> *You can't change a person's heart, but you can allow me to soften yours when working through disagreements.*

PUSH OUT DEEPER: Luke 17:3–4; Mark 11:25; 2 Corinthians 2:7; Ephesians 4:32

Increase

The apostles said to the Lord, "Increase our faith!"

LUKE 17:5 NIV

THE EARLY FOLLOWERS of Jesus meet their shortcomings on a regular basis. They slam into their inability to forgive. They have to climb over feelings. The apostles clamor around the Lord after hearing the teaching of the stumbling block.

This is hard!

Increase our faith, Lord.

What a powerful plea. Rather than asking Jesus to remove the stumbling block or fix a situation or person, they ask for increased faith. Sure, they are aware of their weaknesses; just as certain, they are aware of his strength in the midst of their shortcomings.

Give us what we need, Lord.

When we place our own hearts before the Lord in a conflict, it's a sign of maturity. We realize what we cannot change, but offer up our own lives for transformation.

> ### Come With Me
> *Sincere and raw prayer is a beautiful way to trust me over your feelings.*

Let's make that our prayer today.

Help us see what we cannot see in the natural.

Move us from short-term feelings to the bigger picture.

Increase our faith, Lord.

Whether or not anyone else is changed, we will not remain untouched.

PUSH OUT DEEPER: Luke 17:5; Philippians 4:13; Ephesians 3:16; 1 Timothy 1:12

In Us

> And the Lord said, "If you had faith like a grain of mustard seed, you could say to this mulberry tree, 'Be uprooted and planted in the sea,' and it would obey you."
>
> LUKE 17:6 ESV

SOME CALL IT a sycamine tree. This tree bears green-yellow figs throughout the growing season. The figs traipse along the trunk and branches, rather than at the end of twigs like other fruit-bearing trees. All it takes for this hardy tree to root and grow is to stick a branch into the soil.

It would be a challenge for anyone to speak to this tree in faith, and for it to uproot and be planted in the sea.

What does this have to do with forgiving an offense?

Jesus is encouraging them to believe in their deep-rooted faith. They've seen miracles and demons routed. This same faith is a powerful force when trying to forgive. The power of God is within them.

> ### Come With Me
> *If you struggle to forgive, come to me. I'll take that seed of faith and produce fruit in you.*

Rather than worry over our inability to forgive, we can go to the Source already living inside us. Our faith is planted as we speak truth to that hurt and release the offense.

PUSH OUT DEEPER: Luke 17:6; John 6:29; 1 John 3:23; 1 John 4:15

Servant-Hearted

"Will he thank the servant because he did what he was told to do?"

LUKE 17:9 NIV

AS THE DISCIPLES PRACTICE the power of their faith, they witness many great things. They walk into a throng of sick people, and many leave healed through their prayers. As they walk through the streets, people gather in multitudes to listen. When they enter a home, they often sit in places of honor.

Sometimes it's a little tricky, because the acts of God are attributed to them. Jesus reminds them—and us—that ministry is not about us. Just as Jesus labored long days and knelt to take sandals from dusty feet, we too are servants. Spiritual pride is a belief that answered prayer or achievements are tied to our own importance. Yet a servant-hearted ministry is about those standing in front of us.

> ### Come With Me
> *A humble-hearted servant keeps her focus on the need before her and her God within. That is a heart I can use greatly.*

As we exercise our faith, we *will* see God at work, yet Jesus served for the joy set before him. As we walk in faith, our reward is fantastic! We are eyewitnesses to faith springing forth in the lives of those around us. People are set free. Families are mended. Sin is conquered. Broken lives are pieced back together—all because of faith in our marvelous Savior.

PUSH OUT DEEPER: Luke 17:7–10; 1 Kings 8:23; John 13:12–15; Acts 3:6–7

Heard

As he was going into a village, ten men who had leprosy met him.
They stood at a distance and called out in a loud voice, "Jesus,
Master, have pity on us!"

LUKE 17:12–13 NIV

THE TEN LEPERS STAND in a cluster of misery. One is a Samaritan. Normally he would not be associated with the other nine, except for the bond of leprosy. This disease has made them outcasts. They are careful not to approach an unafflicted person, but they dare to call out Jesus' name. There's hope in this scene unfolding on the border of Galilee and Samaria as the lepers dare to believe Jesus will hear their plea.

> **Come With Me**
> *Offer dignity and hope
> to that one whose
> world is far from safe.*

What courage. What bravery! What faith!

They shout and Jesus hears.

There are women across the world who stand at a distance. They are enslaved. They are without access to clean water. They are denied education. They are stricken with poverty. They are loved by God fiercely.

Will we hear their pleas?

Will we respond?

As we follow Jesus, may our ears become open to the pleas of those afflicted and calling for help. May their voices be heard as we swiftly respond in Jesus' name.

PUSH OUT DEEPER: Luke 17:11–13; Psalm 82:4; Proverbs 24:11; Isaiah 58:6

Pure Praise

Jesus asked, "Weren't ten men made clean? Where are the other nine?"

LUKE 17:17 GW

JESUS TOLD THE LEPERS to go straightaway to the priest. As they travel, one notices his skin turning from diseased to brand-new. Another feels his face, and the portions where skin had fallen away are plump and full. Imagine their celebration as they leap and dance into the courtyard of the temple! Only one, however, finds his way back to Jesus. The Samaritan thanks him for his renewed life.

Jesus searches the road behind the man.

Weren't there ten?

The lepers obeyed Jesus by going to the priest, but only one thanked him for healing his body. Certainly the other nine were grateful, but the Samaritan turned thanksgiving into pure praise as he stood before the Healer.

Come With Me

When you praise me for answered prayers, it builds your faith and it makes my heart glad.

If we were to go back over the last ten years, or the last ten days, how many prayers have we presented to our heavenly Father? In response, we were offered wisdom. Guidance and comfort. Perhaps a miracle. Maybe we are grateful, but do we pause to thank him for those answered prayers, or do we continue on our way? Let us express pure praise for answered prayer, long before we bring the next request.

PUSH OUT DEEPER: Luke 17:14–18; Psalm 100:1; Psalm 98:8; Psalm 109:30

Go Your Way

And he said to him, "Arise, go your way. Your faith has made you well."

LUKE 17:19 NKJV

NINE OF THE LEPERS leave the temple. They are all healed. They are all released back to their families and jobs and communities. Every boundary is demolished as they reenter society. Nonetheless, Jesus gives this grateful man one more gift.

Arise.

He has fallen on his face before the Lord. Jesus bids him to rise, and they stand eye to eye, the depths of Jesus' love reflected in his face. Certainly his skin is restored, but so is his soul.

Go your way.

The leper obeys Jesus by going to the priest, but he seeks the signature of a life marked by Jesus. He is free to go his way as a man of faith, changed from that day forward.

> **Come With Me**
> *Don't just ask me to change your situation; invite me to change you.*

Your faith has made you whole.

Nine lepers walked away with brand-new skin, but only one leaves with a brand-new life. God offers each of us more than a new set of circumstances. He invites us to arise as his daughters, go our way with purpose, and live as one healed from the inside out.

PUSH OUT DEEPER: Luke 17:19; 2 Corinthians 3:3; Ezekiel 36:26; Psalm 40:8

Heart Work

> Being asked by the Pharisees when the kingdom of God would come, he answered them, "The kingdom of God is not coming in ways that can be observed."
>
> LUKE 17:20 ESV

THEY HAVE HAD ENOUGH OF JESUS' "non-king-like" behavior, looking out for the downtrodden and praying for people until the sun goes down. The Pharisees are ready for the kingdom of God to come, at least the kingdom they envision.

The kingdom of God won't come in ways that can be observed.

It isn't Jesus' first time to correct their assumptions. The kingdom wouldn't come through war or unrest. It would emerge as people came into relationship with God almighty.

Come With Me
When you follow me closely in your everyday life, it builds my kingdom.

This is heart work. It is also hard work, for it is deeper than changing laws or confronting authority; it is more about self-denial and loving others.

We might despair over the state of our culture, our communities, or our church and desire to confront or condemn. True kingdom work is much subtler. We follow Jesus' example: loving the downtrodden, living with integrity, our words and actions marked by character and compassion.

When we do the heart work, the kingdom work in our communities, churches, and culture begins.

PUSH OUT DEEPER: Luke 17:20–21; John 18:36; Psalm 25:21; Romans 14:17

169

Ransomed

> "But first the Son of Man must suffer terribly and be rejected by this generation."
>
> LUKE 17:25 NLT

NO KING WOULD WILLINGLY SUFFER as Jesus will in the days ahead. Kings were captured and even killed by their enemies, but this King isn't to be arrested and tried. He plans to offer himself up as a ransom for many. He is greater than his enemy, but his greatest strength is surrendering to God's plan for mankind. Jesus already knows every violent word, every drop of spittle, every strike of the cat-o'-nine-tails, and every painful indentation from the crown of thorns upon his brow.

He knows, but he doesn't turn away.

The kingdom of God is among the disciples, but they don't recognize him. Do we? Jesus suffered terribly for us. He felt every lash. He heard every word of judgment. He agonized as the brunt of our sin weighed upon his body.

> **Come With Me**
> *Take the bread, remember my broken body. Take the cup, remember my blood shed for you.*

The kingdom of God lives among us.

The kingdom of God lives *in* us.

Every time we remember his sacrifice, we tell him it was worth it. We cannot imagine his suffering, but let us not fail to thank him for paying the price that set us free.

PUSH OUT DEEPER: Luke 17:22–25; Isaiah 53:5; 1 Peter 3:18; John 6:33

Jesus Will Return

"Yes, it will be 'business as usual' right up to the day when the
Son of Man is revealed."

LUKE 17:30 NLT

HIS JOURNEY WILL NOT END at the tomb. Jesus, having faithfully carried out the instructions of his heavenly Father, will return to take his rightful place with him. He has taught this truth in parables, revealing truth through stories that meet the disciples right where they are. He has spoken plainly, even as he notes the confused looks on the disciples' faces.

I will return.

This is his promise. We have heard the words repeatedly, but do we comprehend?

Jesus will return.

> ### Come With Me
> *See the signs? I
> will return.*

Will he find us doing "business as usual," or will he find us ready? Certainly he will find us working or sleeping or tending that little one. Surely we'll be in fields or in high-rise buildings or sitting in a pew at church.

It's not where we are, but what we are anticipating.

It's not what we are doing, but why we do it.

It's not who we are with, but what is within.

Jesus will return.

Will we be ready?

PUSH OUT DEEPER: Luke 17:26–30; John 14:2; Acts 1:11; Hebrews 9:28

What Will Matter

"Whoever tries to keep their life will lose it, and whoever loses their life will preserve it."

LUKE 17:33 NIV

IKE LIGHTNING FLASHING ACROSS THE SKY, Jesus' return to earth will be glorious. It will be visible, sudden, and unexpected. When he arrives, those seemingly very important things that occupied a person's time or thoughts will hold little value. There will be things that stole our time, and even our hearts, that will seem trivial. There will be moments that hold eternal significance.

What if we examined our lives now, while there is time?

It's a gift to enjoy life! We are blessed with the beauty of creation, with relationships with those we love, with purpose, and with knowing our Savior. Let's also be truthful about those things we crave or pursue that take us away from God's best. May we be honest about the hours, days, and even years we spend chasing those things that steal from us in the end.

Jesus asked his disciples to release their life to the Lord.

Every part of it.

He is faithful to show us what to hold on to and what to let go. Following Jesus now enriches not only our present life but our eternal life. For on that day, knowing Jesus is all that will matter.

> **Come With Me**
> *Denying self is seen as negative, and yet it's how you find your real self.*

PUSH OUT DEEPER: Luke 17:31–37; Philippians 3:7; John 3:30; Acts 20:24

Lifeline

Then Jesus told his disciples a parable to show them that they should always pray and not give up.

LUKE 18:1 NIV

JUST AS FOOD AND WINE keep their bodies healthy, prayer is a lifeline for the disciples. Jesus is pouring words over his friends. They depend on him. They allow him to take the lead. The thought of traveling as they have been, of long days of ministry, of persecution without the physical presence of Jesus is more than they can comprehend.

They *can* do it, but not without their lifeline.

Prayer will keep them connected to Jesus. Jesus will not be with them in person, yet he'll be with them everywhere they go, no matter what they are doing and what they are feeling. Just as they sat with him on a mountainside, they will always be able to talk to him.

Prayer is our lifeline.

> ## Come With Me
>
> *As with bread and water, you are nourished as you pray. Talk to me throughout your day; invite me into every part of your life.*

There are times we won't hear the voice of God, but that doesn't mean he isn't listening. We may not feel his presence, but that doesn't mean he isn't near.

He's with us always.

That's his pledge to us, that when we talk with him, he hears every last word.

PUSH OUT DEEPER: Luke 18:1; Ephesians 6:18; Acts 1:14; 1 Thessalonians 5:17

Opposite

He said, "In a city there was a judge who didn't fear God or respect people. In that city there was also a widow who kept coming to him and saying, 'Give me justice.'"

LUKE 18:2–3 GW

THE JUDGE RULES over his territory. He is arrogant and disrespectful to God and man. Unfortunately, this judge is the widow's only avenue to justice. She comes to him once, then again. He ignores her. She comes to him repeatedly until the judge tires of her. In order to shut her up, he takes up her case.

Jesus, in some of his parables, contrasted man's nature with God's.

The judge failed to respect God or this woman, but our heavenly Father's nature is love. When we bring our heartaches to him, he hears us.

When we are bruised and treated unfairly, it grieves our God, for he despises evil. Our Lord's character is the opposite of this judge, yet we often approach God as if he's the same. He will never be unaware of or indifferent to our prayers, for his nature is intimacy with those who call upon his name.

> **Come With Me**
> Your prayers have been heard. I am working in ways you cannot see, battling on your behalf.

God is true to the Word.

Come freely is what Scripture says.

Come boldly is our invitation.

Come quickly, for he is waiting.

PUSH OUT DEEPER: Luke 18:2–8; Daniel 10:12; Psalm 102:17; Psalm 22:24

Virtue

> "And the tax collector, standing afar off, would not so much as raise
> his eyes to heaven, but beat his breast, saying, 'God, be merciful
> to me a sinner!'"
>
> LUKE 18:13 NKJV

THE SELF-RIGHTEOUS MAN CLOSES his eyes and lifts his chin to pray.
He lists his good qualities. He itemizes all the things he does right.
God, I thank you that I am not like other people.

Not far away stands a second man. Perhaps he's the very one the
self-righteous man describes. He lists none of the merits the first man
shares with such detail. His eyes are downcast. His
hands strike his chest in a show of remorse. He
doesn't list his virtues to God; he relies on God's
virtue to save his soul.

Both may be leaders. Both may have families. The distinction is not in accomplishments
or reputation, but in their individual approaches
to God. One is occupied with himself, and another immersed in God,
reaching for mercy.

Self-righteousness is as filthy rags, yet we are tempted to hold them
up as if they are beautiful. Our works are an outward demonstration of
faith, but they do not reflect the inward state of our hearts. Only God
sees that. Rather than list our virtues to a God who sees all, we rely on
God's virtue to redeem us when we fall short.

> **Come With Me**
> *Humility stands up
> to self-righteousness
> and calls its bluff.*

PUSH OUT DEEPER: Luke 18:9–13; Proverbs 15:33; Philippians 2:3; James 3:13

Answered Prayer

"I tell you that this man, rather than the other, went home justified before God. For all those who exalt themselves will be humbled, and those who humble themselves will be exalted."

LUKE 18:14 NIV

THE SELF-RIGHTEOUS MAN LIVES a life of good works. He tithes. He prays. He is free of scandalous or public sins. The publican's sin is a burden so heavy he strikes his fists against his chest in shame.

Only one prayer receives an answer that day.

The self-righteous man's words are a recital of his goodness, but not really a prayer. Perhaps, because he's in the temple, his recital is for the ears of nearby priests or religious leaders.

The other—in spite of his sin—left with his burden removed.

> ### Come With Me
> I already know your struggles as well as your heart. Come as you are and let's talk.

What is in this story for us?

God knows who we are. We don't have to introduce ourselves or our works. We don't have to prove how good we are or that we've earned the right to be called a child of God. There are no masks. No points earned.

We simply come as we are. In humility, we understand that God knows us.

Every mistake. Every battle. Every ill motivation. He sees our desire to please him and to submit to his guidance. We strip our prayers of self-righteousness, but also of guilt as we ask for and receive mercy.

PUSH OUT DEEPER: Luke 18:14; Proverbs 29:23; 1 Peter 5:5–6; Psalm 138:6

Get Out of the Way

Now they were bringing even infants to him that he might touch them. And when the disciples saw it, they rebuked them.

LUKE 18:15 ESV

PETER, ANDREW, BARTHOLOMEW, AND OTHERS hover around Jesus. He's been telling them something big is ahead, something unpleasant. In their love for him, their protective instincts kick in when parents start to bring their little ones to Jesus.

> ### Come With Me
> That work I've begun in that child's heart is genuine. Listen and affirm that tender shoot of faith.

He's tired.

He's determined to go to Jerusalem. We've got to go!

He's already prayed for the adults. Why bother the teacher with mere children?

Jesus is angry and rebukes them.

Don't get in their way.

A child's tender heart is receptive to the Savior. We can downplay a child's response to faith, telling them they are too young to know of such deep matters. We can be guilty of speaking ill of other believers in their presence. We can fail to understand that Jesus longs to lead and love that child.

Don't get in their way.

Let's break down any barrier, so that a child feels safe to run into his arms.

PUSH OUT DEEPER: Luke 18:15–16; Joel 1:3; Exodus 13:8; Deuteronomy 11:18

Open Arms

> "Truly, I say to you, whoever does not receive the kingdom of God like a child shall not enter it."
>
> LUKE 18:17 ESV

JESUS TAKES THE LITTLE CHILDREN into his arms, puts his hands on them, and blesses them. Are they aware this is the Son of God? Not likely.

Do they understand fully the blessing they receive?

Not at all.

All they know is that they are welcome. There is no bargaining for his favor. There is no reservation. As children, they clamber near Jesus or tell him a story. Perhaps one shows him a pretty rock found in the road while another touches Jesus' cheek.

Jesus banished the barricades between these children and himself. He broke down every barrier between mankind and our heavenly Father.

We are welcome to approach Jesus as though his arms are open wide. We are asked to receive the gift of relationship, and to unwrap and enjoy this priceless gift we've been given.

Let us come to Jesus as children, our souls unguarded and open.

Come With Me
Behold what manner of love my Father has lavished on you as his daughter.

PUSH OUT DEEPER: Luke 18:17; Psalm 19:7; Psalm 119:98; 1 Corinthians 4:17

One Thing

> When Jesus heard this, he said to him, "One thing you still lack.
> Sell all that you have and distribute to the poor, and you will have
> treasure in heaven; and come, follow me."
>
> LUKE 18:22 ESV

JESUS LOOKS UPON THE YOUNG MAN and loves him, for he desires to do the right thing. In response to his question, Jesus tells him to sell everything he owns and give it to the poor.

Sadly, it's the one thing he's not willing to give up. More importantly, it's the one thing he lacks. He knows how to live a moral life, but he doesn't know how to give Jesus his all.

Come With Me

When I ask you to release that one thing, it is to give you what you really need.

Nothing we hold on to compares with Jesus. Our greatest asset is our one-to-one relationship with him. Money was never the issue with the rich young ruler, the lack Jesus saw in him is the real story.

When we release our hold, we discover what we have been missing all along.

Heavenly Father, what we hold on to is what defines us. We present to you all that we have been holding so tightly. It was yours from the beginning. Take it. In its place we hold on to joy. We hold on to laughter. We hold on to second chances. We hold on to kindness. We hold on to loving other people well. We hold on to you.

PUSH OUT DEEPER: Luke 18:18–22; Mark 10:21; 1 Timothy 6:17; Proverbs 11:28

Our Identity

Jesus looked at him and said, "How hard it is for the rich to enter the kingdom of God!"

LUKE 18:24 NIV

JESUS IS ATTIRED IN A SIMPLE ROBE, while the rich young ruler is clothed in purple. Jesus has no earthly home, while the rich young ruler lives in luxury. The young man recognizes goodness in Jesus, but his good life is where he feels comfortable.

How hard it is for the rich to enter the kingdom of God.

Jesus' words are sorrowful. The rich young man's identity is in what he owns and what he does, rather than in the riches of the kingdom.

Is it even possible to identify with the rich young ruler? The *rich* are other people. They live in large houses and drive expensive cars and have major bank accounts. But in a world where so many don't have access to clean water, shelter, medical care, food, or even safety, if we have those things, we *are* the rich young ruler in this story. Jesus' question is just as much for us as it was for him.

> ### Come With Me
> *What I offer you cannot be stored here on earth.*

How do we identify ourselves? Is it in what we own? Is it in our reputation?

He asks that we give everything, beginning with ourselves, in order that we might discover our true identity.

PUSH OUT DEEPER: Luke 18:23–25; Daniel 12:3; 1 Corinthians 15:42; Revelation 3:17

Pruning the Vine

Jesus said to them, "I can guarantee this truth: Anyone who gave up his home, wife, brothers, parents, or children because of God's kingdom will certainly receive many times as much in this life and will receive eternal life in the world to come."

LUKE 18:29–30 GW

HIGH ALTITUDE AND RICH SOIL make this part of the country a nearly perfect setting for vineyards. In the summer season, workers harvest grapes, olives, dates, figs, pomegranates, and numerous other fruits. If the grapevines are not pruned in winter, they will grow lush vines but bear little fruit.

It's hard to envision that such severe pruning is the best for these vines. Without their hearty canes, they appear desolate. But without this step they will never reach their potential.

The pruning process leaves us feeling exposed, perhaps abandoned, unsure.

When God prunes feelings, things, or anything we hold dear, it's to give God first place in those relationships and in those feelings.

This bears fruit in our faith. It creates a harvest in our lives and within our relationships. After a season of pruning, our lives bear fruit, not only in this season but for eternity.

> ### Come With Me
> As I prune you, trust me. I desire that your life produce an abundant harvest.

PUSH OUT DEEPER: Luke 18:26–30; Hosea 4:6–7; Zechariah 8:12; Matthew 6:33

Fulfilled

"For he will be delivered over to the Gentiles and will be mocked and shamefully treated and spit upon."

LUKE 18:32 ESV

SIMILAR TO OLD LETTERS shut away in a box, the writings of the prophets are lovely to read but don't seem to connect to present times. Jesus blows dust from the words as he turns toward Jerusalem. He draws the original twelve close. They are the ones who know him best. They are the chosen, those who will take the church to the next generation.

He reminds them of the prophets' words.

I'll be delivered to the Gentiles, just as they foretold.

I'll be mocked and shamefully treated.

I'll die a painful death, but death will not hold me.

Generations after the prophets left earth, Jesus fulfilled their words.

He left heaven to rescue us from sin. He was despised, smitten, rejected. He opened his arms and lay on a rugged cross, and three days later he rose again.

> ### Come With Me
> *Ask the Holy Spirit to bring my Word to life within you.*

We can trust the Word of God. The truth within—from the story of Jesus' love to his return one day—is more than a collection of dusty letters.

They are life! They run to us, they change us, they show us the way.

PUSH OUT DEEPER: Luke 18:31–34; 1 Peter 1:10–11; 2 Peter 1:21; Isaiah 53:4–5

Son of David

They told him that Jesus the Nazarene was going by.

LUKE 18:37 NLT

A BLIND MAN HEARS FEET tramping nearby. What is the commotion? When he learns it is Jesus the Nazarene, the blind man leaps to his feet and shouts.

Jesus, son of David, have mercy on me!

There are many who shout out Jesus' name, but this is different.

Jesus, son of David, have mercy on me!

> **Come With Me**
> *Your cry of confidence reaches all the way to the throne.*

The man's cry is more than a desperate call for help, it's a proclamation of faith! Surely he not only has heard about Jesus' miracles, but believes. His appeal is not to Jesus the Nazarene but to Jesus the Messiah, son of David. The blind man understands who is nearby and will not stop crying out until Jesus is standing in front of him.

What faith! What courage!

May we approach Jesus in the same manner. When we call out Jesus' name in faith, our appeal is not in vain. We are placing our trust in Jesus, son of David.

Messiah. Savior. Healer. Redeemer. Anointed one.

As we pray in faith, Jesus is near and our faith is sweet incense to our Lord.

PUSH OUT DEEPER: Luke 18:35–38; Revelation 8:3; James 1:6; James 5:15

Clamor

And immediately he received his sight, and followed him, glorifying God: and all the people, when they saw it, gave praise unto God.

LUKE 18:43 KJV

SEVERAL PEOPLE TURN at the sound of the blind man's wail. They wave their hands at him, demanding he soften his plea. He cries out louder. They try to shush him. The blind man is lowly, most likely poor. He may even be a beggar. How dare he intrude upon such a man as Jesus the Nazarene!

Note how different Jesus' response is to this man.

He stops and asks that he be brought to him. He inquires about his need, and within minutes the blind man can see. The blind man is not the only one whose eyes are opened that day. When everyone sees the miracle, they give praise to Jesus.

We are often told to keep our prayers to ourselves. It's okay to pray in private, but praying for someone publicly is seen as less than acceptable or somehow wrong. As a result, even as we notice the plight of another soul, we may feel awkward offering to pray.

> ## Come With Me
> *Even those who clamor the loudest against prayer search for hope in desperate places. Listen for my voice, and I'll show you what to do.*

Jesus shows us what is acceptable. Look past the noise of rebuke to see the person and their need, and pray for those seeking hope.

PUSH OUT DEEPER: Luke 18:39–43; Acts 28:8; Acts 4:14; Acts 3:7

Just for One

Jesus entered Jericho and made his way through the town.

LUKE 19:1 NLT

JESUS TRAVELS THROUGH JERICHO, making his way through the town. Jericho has a bad reputation, and some describe it as evil. It is filled with publicans and sinners, but also priests.

The highway between Jericho and Jerusalem is considered unsafe. Jesus once told a parable about a Samaritan beaten and left for dead on this very road. There are other routes. Safer roads. His followers follow him, not realizing there is a reason for the detour.

There's a man ahead; he'll be in a tree.

Jesus has an appointment he will not miss.

When we pray for certain loved ones, we may despair at where sin takes them.

> **Come With Me**
> *The darker the pit, the greater my light shines.*

Jesus doesn't shy away from darkness, for he is light.

He doesn't shy away from broken humanity, for he is hope.

He battled hell and won, and there's no place our loved ones can go that is beyond his reach.

We won't give up, because Jesus is on the way. He blazes the darkness to reclaim them.

PUSH OUT DEEPER: Luke 19:1; Revelation 1:18; Matthew 16:19; Isaiah 41:14

Come and Dine

When Jesus came to the tree, he looked up and said, "Zacchaeus, come down! I must stay at your house today."

LUKE 19:5 GW

ROMAN TAX COLLECTORS are assigned a region. Their job is to collect taxes from citizens in that area. A tax collector is paid a sufficient income, but authorities look the other way if a tax collector pads his income through extortion.

A little here. A lot there. This practice makes many tax collectors wealthy, but it is reviled and feared.

Zacchaeus is looking for Jesus because he's curious. He may not know much about Jesus, but Jesus knows everything about the man sitting in the sycamore-fig tree.

> **Come With Me**
> *I'm going to dine with you today and every day.*

He approaches him and asks him to come down from the tree. In a bold move, Jesus invites himself to dinner. Zacchaeus has no idea of the life change he is about to experience.

Jesus asks to dine with us.

In our home. In our heart. In our workplace. In the dark of night when we struggle to sleep.

When we say yes to that invitation, we are changed because of it.

Jesus, you are asking to be a part of every aspect of our lives. We say yes!

PUSH OUT DEEPER: Luke 19:2–6; Revelation 3:20; John 21:12–15; Matthew 9:10–12

Recompense

Meanwhile, Zacchaeus stood before the Lord and said, "I will give half my wealth to the poor, Lord, and if I have cheated people on their taxes, I will give them back four times as much!"

LUKE 19:8 NLT

WE DON'T HEAR THE CONVERSATION around the table, but Zacchaeus is transformed after that conversation. He promises to give half of his wealth to the poor, and to recompense four times the amount to those he cheated. This is a typical sentence levied on a thief under Roman law. No one has accused Zacchaeus; he joyfully makes his wrongs right all on his own.

> **Come With Me**
>
> *If you are in the wrong, make your wrong right. Even if it is not accepted, it's beautiful in my sight.*

Very few of us want to wrong someone, but we all do at some point.

When that wrong is brought into the open, we may want to defend ourselves. We may want to explain that we didn't realize it was a wrong. We were joking. We were kidding. We go into self-protection mode, failing to see the growth opportunity of saying we are sorry.

What if we offered immediate restitution for a wrong? Rather than an excuse, we offer a sincere apology. Rather than defending our actions, we listen to the one we hurt. We make amends before making a case for ourselves. We right the wrong rather than just being *right*.

This is where our heart makeover begins.

PUSH OUT DEEPER: Luke 19:7–8; Leviticus 25:17; Jeremiah 7:5; 2 Corinthians 7:10

Seek and Save

"For the Son of Man came to seek and to save the lost."

LUKE 19:10 ESV

WE AREN'T PRIVY to the rest of the conversation between Zacchaeus and Jesus, but we are witnesses to the result. Salvation came to Zacchaeus's house. Jesus sought him, and that ended in redemption.

That's one chapter.

Another began as Zacchaeus gave half of his wealth to feed the poor. He paid back four times what he extorted. Imagine the surprise when he knocked on the door, holding a bag of coins and sharing his story of meeting Jesus.

That led to a third chapter. How many were converted because of Zacchaeus? What did his co-workers say at this change of heart? We have no idea how far-reaching Zacchaeus's salvation story became.

> **Come With Me**
> I came to save the world. Will you tell one of them what I did for you?

Jesus came to seek and save the lost, and one of them was in a tree. Zacchaeus didn't just receive salvation, he acted on it, and that wrote new chapters. In his life, yes, but also in the lives of others.

Jesus, you have saved us. You sought us. Show us the one person who needs to hear our story. If we've done wrong in the past and it hurt someone, show us how to right that wrong. Perhaps that apology will begin a new chapter for them, but it certainly writes a new story in our hearts.

PUSH OUT DEEPER: Luke 19:9–10; John 4:7; John 6:40; Mark 2:15–17

A Vast Kingdom

"A certain nobleman went into a far country to receive for himself
a kingdom and to return."

LUKE 19:12 NKJV

THE DISCIPLES ARE FOCUSED on a lost cause. Jesus redirects them
to see a lost generation.

In this parable, Jesus describes a nobleman who travels to a distant
city to establish his kingdom. The nobleman, who is in line for the
throne, must first seek favor from a higher authority, such as a Roman
emperor. This is a customary practice, with which
Jesus' listeners are familiar. Herod the Great went
on a similar expedition at the time of Jesus' birth.

This meeting will influence how much or how
little territory the nobleman's kingdom covers.

Jesus is alluding to his own deity. He was sent
to a far country to map out a kingdom. God
clearly set the boundaries of that kingdom—every corner of the world,
every person. Jesus was sent to conquer principalities and powers. He
was given authority over every high place and every low valley.

Every person, every country, every tribe in the world is valued territory to our Savior. He redirects our attention from personal, cultural,
or doctrinal interpretations of his mission to show us the world, one
person at a time.

> **Come With Me**
> *I see every person, every
> nation, every inch of
> the world as valuable.*

PUSH OUT DEEPER: Luke 19:11–12; John 1:14; 1 Timothy 6:15; Revelation 17:14

— 189 —

Be My King

> "The citizens of his own country hated him. They sent representatives to follow him and say to the person who was going to appoint him, 'We don't want this man to be our king.'"
>
> LUKE 19:14 GW

THE NOBLEMAN SET OUT on his journey, and citizens sent people to follow him. These men will rush to tell the higher authorities, "We don't want this man to be our king."

We hear the grief in Jesus' voice as he tells this story.

There is growing hostility toward the Messiah among many religious leaders. Jesus feels it when he speaks in the temple. It is the undercurrent as he dines with publicans and those who are lost. If Jesus were to exert power over the people, rather than use his power to heal, he might be more easily accepted.

We may not always appreciate our king.

We want him to tell us what to do, rather than empower us to make our choices. We want him to conquer our enemies, rather than tell us to love them.

> ### Come With Me
> *Many hate me, even today, which makes your unreserved love and obedience an offering.*

As our king, he doesn't dominate or dictate, but places the decision to love and obey in our hands.

PUSH OUT DEEPER: Luke 19:13–14; Mark 12:33; 1 Samuel 15:22; Revelation 19:16

Equal Opportunity

> "He was made king, however, and returned home. Then he sent for the servants to whom he had given the money, in order to find out what they had gained with it."
>
> LUKE 19:15 NIV

TEN SERVANTS WERE EACH GIVEN A POUND to invest during the nobleman's absence. When he returned, he sent for those servants, asking what they had done with the pound in his absence.

Unlike other parables, this is not about a diversity of gifts. It is about equal opportunity. They all have the same amount of money and time.

One increased his pound ten times over and was given authority over ten cities. Another increased his pound five times over and was given authority over five cities. One held up his pound, secured in a handkerchief. He trembled, so afraid his master would be stern with him if he lost it or spent it in the wrong way that he kept the one pound hidden away.

Jesus is temporarily away but promises to return.

We have all been given the same amount of time and the same message that changes lives.

We have equal opportunity to use what God has given us in greater measure. Jesus is not a taskmaster, but rather invests in us that we might invest in others so that the dividends add up—in lives, in answered prayer, and in acts of mercy over the world around us.

> **Come With Me**
> *Your faithfulness with small things opens doors to even more territory.*

PUSH OUT DEEPER: Luke 19:16–21; Proverbs 27:18; 2 Kings 12:14–15; 1 Corinthians 4:2

Reunion

> "'And as for these enemies of mine who didn't want me to be their king—bring them in and execute them right here in front of me.'"
>
> LUKE 19:27 NLT

WHEN THE NOBLEMAN RETURNS, he calls his servants together. The servants who rushed to tarnish his name lose everything. The servants who increased his wealth while he was gone are rewarded. The servant who didn't increase the pound is not given additional territory, but he remains in the house of the king.

Some are blessed by his return. Others face judgment.

One day we'll account for our lives. For many, it will be a glorious reunion. Some will weep as a lustrous crown is placed on their head, realizing how they impacted eternity here on earth. Others will mourn missed opportunities, but they will rejoice at his mercy as they step into the Father's house.

> ### Come With Me
> *I desire that none should perish, but that all will be with me in eternity.*

Sadly, that leaves those who only now acknowledge that Jesus is Lord yet had rebuked, rejected, and refused him all of their days.

Jesus didn't come to condemn, but to save.

He longs to rescue all of us, even those who reject him.

While we have breath, let's receive his love and call him our Lord, King of Kings.

PUSH OUT DEEPER: Luke 19:22–28; John 3:17; 2 Corinthians 5:10; Hebrews 9:27–28

Triumphal Entry

He said to them, "Go into the village ahead of you. As you enter, you will find a young donkey tied there. No one has ever sat on it. Untie it, and bring it."

LUKE 19:30 GW

JESUS TELLS THE DISCIPLES to go into the village. There they will find a young donkey colt tethered. They are to loose his halter and bring him to Jesus.

His triumphal entry will be on a donkey, just as Zechariah the prophet prophesied generations earlier.

> ## Come With Me
> *My suffering was never in vain, but that sin might be broken over your life.*

His followers have begged him to act like a king, yet Jesus has never drawn attention to himself. On this day, however, Jesus acts as a king. We may see a donkey as a lowly animal, but kings often chose a donkey colt for their entrance.

It's not his ride that's humble. It's the man sitting atop of it who is the ultimate display of humility. He puts his heels in the colt's flanks and starts down. Jerusalem is his end destination on earth, but it's also a beginning.

It is the beginning of suffering. It is the beginning of betrayal. It is the beginning of persecution for his followers that will span for years afterward.

When he threw his leg over the donkey, he chose to suffer—even for those who will reject him all the way to the cross. How great the manner of love God lavished on us, suffering to break the stronghold of sin.

PUSH OUT DEEPER: Luke 19:29–30; Zechariah 9:9; Mark 11:9; 1 Peter 2:23

193

Am I Ready?

"If anyone asks you, 'Why are you untying it?' you shall say this: 'The Lord has need of it.'"

LUKE 19:31 ESV

A MOTHER DONKEY AND A COLT are tied for safety's sake. The colt has never been ridden, and surely feels safe by its mother's side. When the owner of the donkeys glances outside, he sees unfamiliar men loosening the ropes. He goes outside to see what is going on.

Hospitality is a trademark, especially during Passover. It's not unusual to share belongings, even something as valuable as a donkey. But this colt isn't ready for riding. Maybe the mother would be a better option.

The disciples insist that Jesus asked for the colt. Donkeys aren't known as submissive animals, yet somehow that colt leaves its mother. It allows disciples to toss garments on its back. It stands patiently as Jesus mounts it and treks down unfamiliar roads amid shouting and waving of palm leaves. What a miracle!

> **Come With Me**
> *If you hear me saying "Now," put it into my care.*

The owner of the colt must have had doubts, but when he realized who was asking for the colt, he let go of his misgivings. If it was for the Master, he'd trust him.

How often do we hold on to something because we think we're not ready, or it's not ready? We want to wait. Finesse it. Perfect it. If Jesus is the one asking, our part is to put it into his care as we trust him to do good with it.

PUSH OUT DEEPER: Luke 19:31; Genesis 5:14; 2 Kings 5:13–14; Nehemiah 2:12

Purple

> And they brought him to Jesus: and they cast their garments upon
> the colt, and they set Jesus thereon.
>
> LUKE 19:35 KJV

THIS ENTRY INTO JERUSALEM is different from any other. The disciples are accustomed to people flocking around Jesus, though he never seeks their adoration. Yet this time Jesus is launching an intricate plan of entry into Jerusalem.

He'll ride in on a colt. He'll sit higher than others, just as royalty would. He'll receive shouts of praise. It's what the disciples have hoped for all along.

They search for something to place on the back of the colt. A king cannot sit on a bare donkey. They don't have purple cloth as befitting a king; all they have are their own robes and cloaks. One disciple removes his cloak and drapes it across the colt's back. Another follows suit. Quickly they all take off their outer cloaks.

> **Come With Me**
> *When you give me all
> of you, it is as precious
> as purple cloth.*

The moment the disciples strip off their cloaks, those outer garments become as precious as purple. Jesus sees straight to their hearts. They love him so much that they don't wait to give him the finest cloth, but give him all they have.

We may be waiting to give our best to Jesus, when all he asks is for what we have right now. We give him our all, and that becomes the best.

PUSH OUT DEEPER: Luke 19:33–35; John 2:9–10; 2 Corinthians 8:12; Mark 12:43

Spontaneous

When he reached the place where the road started down the Mount
of Olives, all of his followers began to shout and sing as they walked
along, praising God for all the wonderful miracles they had seen.

LUKE 19:37 NLT

THE MESSIAH STARTS DOWN THE MOUNT, a crowd bustling
beside him. Spontaneous song breaks out in celebration. Followers
dance beside the donkey, their voices lifted in praise and excitement.

Jerusalem is a city of Roman rulers and officers, Hebrew teachers
and scribes. What will they think when Jesus enters the city gates in
such a noisy display? One group might scoff at
their ragtag appearance. Others may wonder at
this new religious movement. There will be one
crowd who knows well the words of Zechariah the
prophet, and they might shudder as they watch
it come true in front of them.

Whether his followers sing because Jesus is
acting as a king, or because they see him as the
Messiah, they don't care about the response of those in the city.

They sing of his miracles as they weave toward them.

What if we broke out into spontaneous praise today?

Jesus is worthy of our worship. Consider his goodness. We don't
need a songbook, for as we think of his love, we cannot help but sing
out his name.

> **Come With Me**
>
> *When you worship
> with no other reason
> but your love for me,
> you find me near.*

PUSH OUT DEEPER: Luke 19:36–38; Psalm 118:22–23; 2 Samuel 6:14; Psalm 87:7

Cry Out

He answered, "I tell you, if these were silent, the very stones would cry out."

LUKE 19:40 ESV

JESUS EMBRACES HIS ROLE as Messiah before embracing his role as the Lamb.

One begins with worship. The other with sorrow.

Ever-present critics tell him to shush his followers, but he refuses. He is the Messiah and spotless Lamb, and heaven and earth cannot help but tremble at his majesty. If the disciples were to be quiet at his triumphal entry, age-old stones in the city gates would cry out in their place.

> ## Come With Me
> *Come. Let us rejoice together at the demise of sin's stranglehold.*

"Hosanna to the King!" is a fit song for the Lamb of God.

He's our Lord, but let us never forget that he's also the Lamb of God.

Our sin was laid upon him. He didn't defend himself, saying not a word. Instead, he saw the cross as a means of liberating us from the curse of sin and death.

Hosanna to the King! Hosanna to the Lamb who gave his life for us!

Savior, we lift our voices to worship with those who ran alongside you. Hosanna to your name! Thank you for your sacrifice. Thank you for having us on your heart as you approached Jerusalem and the cross.

PUSH OUT DEEPER: Luke 19:39–40; Habakkuk 2:11; Psalm 96:11; Revelation 15:3

A King Weeps

As he approached Jerusalem and saw the city, he wept over it.

LUKE 19:41 NIV

JESUS' CHEST HEAVES as he takes in the city below. He isn't weeping at his upcoming misery, but in sorrow for those who have rejected him.

He is a King in search of a lost sheep who wandered out of the fold.

He is a King in search of a lost coin in the house of God.

He is a King in search of a prodigal son, standing at a distance ashamed.

He is a King who weeps.

Though many have been found, more remain lost.

Our King is keenly aware of that loved one running from his faith. He is pursuing that one in church, struggling to find where she fits. He waits for that prodigal whose shame has kept him far from home.

> ### Come With Me
> *I know you love that one. I do too.*

Our King weeps.

We are not alone in our sorrow, but find hope as Jesus continues to walk the fences searching for that lost sheep, as he sweeps to recover that lost coin, and as he stands in the drive with his arms open wide for the prodigal.

PUSH OUT DEEPER: Luke 19:41–44; John 11:33; Ezekiel 33:11; Psalm 51:17

Holy

> Jesus went into the temple courtyard and began to throw out those
> who were selling things there.
>
> LUKE 19:45 GW

MONEYCHANGERS STAND IN STALLS transacting business. Sacrifices must be purchased. Foreign currency needs to be exchanged. Transactions are customary, especially during Passover, because pilgrims have traveled long distances to participate in this holy event.

Jesus stands at the gates to the temple, distressed.

Salesmen clamor for pilgrims' coins. They shout over each other, vying for business. Stalls normally are set up in the surrounding areas, but these encroach on the outer courts of the temple.

You have turned this into a den of thieves.

As Jesus often does, he has peered to the heart beneath. What he finds are thieves who care less about sacrifices or people than about padding their purses. Jesus clears the men from their stalls. Tables fly. Hawkers leap in surprise, not anticipating Jesus' righteous anger.

Come With Me
Reflect my name with honesty in all you do.

A building isn't sacred, but the presence of God within that dwelling is. Jesus makes his home in us, so wherever we go it can be a holy place. Let's leave personal agendas behind. May Jesus peer into our motives—wherever we might be—and find a heart that longs to lift up and reflect his holy name.

PUSH OUT DEEPER: Luke 19:45–46; Isaiah 56:7; 1 Corinthians 11:20–22; Jeremiah 7:11

199
Spiritual Eyes

> But they could think of nothing, because all the people hung on every word he said.
>
> LUKE 19:48 NLT

JESUS HAS ONE WEEK remaining on earth. What if those around him knew that, especially his critics? Perhaps they would listen more carefully. They'd watch his example more closely. They don't see the signs all around them. They aren't connecting unfolding prophecies to current events.

They scratch their heads in frustration, because all they can think about are their own plans and their own agendas.

We might criticize these men who are so blind, except we can be just as unseeing. Jesus promised he will return for us. He will bid those who call him Lord to celebrate for eternity.

Do we see the sign?

Do we observe the unfolding prophecies around us?

Holy Spirit, we desire spiritual ears to tune in to your voice. We long for spiritual eyes to see the signs. Though we live in tumultuous times, you will show us the way. One day Jesus will return. That's a certainty. Thank you for pointing to his impending return.

Come With Me

As your spiritual eyes are opened, my child, it leads not to apprehension but to anticipation of eternity with me.

PUSH OUT DEEPER: Luke 19:47–48; John 20:30; Jude 1:18; Acts 2:17–18

A Question

"Tell us, by what authority are You doing these things? Or who is he who gave You this authority?"

LUKE 20:2 NKJV

HE ISN'T A RABBI, not in the earthly sense. He isn't a government official. Jesus isn't a scribe.

Who gives you authority to do these things?

This is a legitimate question according to the chief priests, scribes, and elders. All "these things" include teaching in the temple, healing on the Sabbath. It includes approaching the city on a colt as followers sing and praise his name.

We are surrounded by those who do not know Jesus or understand the depths of our faith.

They may question why we pray or why we believe a certain way. Some of the questions come from a hidden place of longing. Others seek a debate. Some desire to silence our faith. Before we can answer their questions, we must understand the answer for ourselves.

Come With Me

Are you living in the authority I have granted?

Our authority comes from heaven. We are invited to follow Jesus. We are charged to fall to our knees in prayer and to share hope with others. We will not abuse that authority, for there is a purpose behind it. We are given authority that we may live our faith so people don't just hear *about* faith, but see that power working in our lives.

PUSH OUT DEEPER: Luke 20:1–2; Matthew 10:1; 1 John 4:4; Romans 16:20

Honest Talk

They discussed it among themselves and said, "If we say, 'From heaven,' he will ask, 'Why didn't you believe him?'"

LUKE 20:5 NIV

I F THE RELIGIOUS LEADERS answer Jesus' question truthfully, they'll corner themselves. If they twist John's words one way or the other to suit their own needs, they'll rouse the anger of the people. Their struggle is not in the choice of their words, but in their motivation. If their motivation were innocent, they wouldn't have to worry over their response.

When we find ourselves stressed to answer a question truthfully, it might be wise to study our motivation.

Are we trying to please someone rather than tell the truth?

Are we trying to put ourselves in the best light?

Are we giving a watered-down version rather than just being open about what took place?

We don't like it when others lie to us, so let's not lie to ourselves.

> ### Come With Me
> If you struggle with what to say and don't know why, ask me to help. We'll go deep to uncover the real issue.

When we find our motivation entwined with emotion, fear, or even impure motives, let's call on the Holy Spirit to untangle those feelings. We can ask for a course correction in our thoughts and our inspiration. When we do that, we don't have to wrestle with words or finagle them to fit a circumstance or a feeling. Instead, we are free to speak the truth, which reflects a heart that reflects our Father.

PUSH OUT DEEPER: Luke 20:3–6; Zechariah 8:16; Ephesians 4:25; Psalm 15:2

Tell Us

Jesus said, "Neither will I tell you by what authority I am doing these things."

LUKE 20:8 NIV

THE MEN WHO INTERRUPT JESUS wear their authority like a sword. They believe they are clever, but Jesus reveals their intentions. They demand that Jesus tell them by whose authority he acts.

Jesus doesn't answer their question directly—because it isn't their real question at all. Their real question is silent. *Why are you threatening our authority?*

Fear drives their crusade. Not righteousness. They are fearful of losing respect among the citizens. They are afraid Jesus will take their place. They are afraid because they speak *about* God, but this one lives as if God is real.

> **Come With Me**
> *Be still and listen.*

At times we don't know what question to ask. We strike in the dark, our feelings leading the way. Even when we are off the mark, we can trust we'll receive a truthful answer.

We ask God if he is present, and he says, "I never left you."

We react in fear, and he says, "Don't be afraid. I am with you."

We demand that God give us what we want, and he says, "Let me show you what you need."

Our heavenly Father will not lead us astray. He understands the question we don't know to ask. He loves us enough to give us the answer.

PUSH OUT DEEPER: Luke 20:7–13; Matthew 6:8; Psalm 38:9; Isaiah 30:21

Fruit

"'What will I do?' the owner asked himself. 'I know! I'll send my cherished son. Surely they will respect him.'"

Luke 20:13 nlt

A T THE END OF THE SEASON the master of the vineyard sends a servant to collect the fruit of the harvest. In a surprising move, the farmers meet the servant and beat him. It's not what the master expected at all. He sends another servant, and yet another—but with the same results.

In a surprising and merciful move, he sends his most valuable representative, his beloved son. They kill him. The farmers cared less about the harvest and their master than about personal gain.

God sent prophets to tell his people about his love. They were beaten, scorned, and persecuted. He sent John the Baptist. He was imprisoned and beheaded. In an act of incredible trust, God sent his Son, Jesus. He came to earth incarnate, a babe born to a virgin.

He too was scorned, beaten, and killed.

We are caretakers, keepers of the harvest.

Jesus will return one day to collect precious fruit. He longs to rejoice over the yield with all of those who work faithfully in the fields.

> **Come With Me**
> *I long that my people care about the harvest, for I will return.*

May we welcome and receive him long before that moment. Let's praise him today for his incredible mercy. Let's thank him for sending a messenger—his beloved Son.

PUSH OUT DEEPER: Luke 20:9–15; Isaiah 5:4; Hebrews 11:36; 2 Chronicles 24:20–21

Crushed

> "Everyone who stumbles over that stone will be broken to pieces, and it will crush anyone it falls on."
>
> LUKE 20:18 NLT

THE RELIGIOUS LEADERS are so angry that they decide to rise against Jesus that very hour. They are frustrated, for Jesus has insinuated that *he* is the beloved son and *they* are the ungrateful farmers.

It is truth, but not a truth they are willing to hear.

They are afraid of riling the crowd, so they scheme to carry out their plans in secret.

They are ruled by their anger. They are employed by their fear.

They have lost their way! These leaders have knowledge at their disposal. They've dissected prophetic teachings and discussed them at length. They are entrusted with the holy of holies. In spite of what they know, fear and anger will crush them as they plot to reduce the Cornerstone to rubble.

Come With Me

Anger isn't an ungodly emotion. It's where it leads you that matters.

Unresolved anger crushes the heart of a believer. When we are frustrated, we too can go to a secret place. There we have the Word at our fingertips. We can drop our burdens in prayer. Instead of being ruled by anger or employed by fear, we find restoration by God's healing spirit.

PUSH OUT DEEPER: Luke 20:16–19; Ephesians 4:31; Psalm 37:8; Colossians 3:8

Sweet Talk

They asked him, "Teacher, we know that you're right in what you
say and teach. Besides, you don't play favorites. Rather, you teach
the way of God truthfully."

LUKE 20:21 GW

SCHEMERS SEND SPIES to question Jesus. They begin with sweet
talk.

Jesus, we know that you teach rightly.

Then they lob a political question.

Everyone is required to pay a tax to the Roman government. Pharisees believe that paying taxes to a pagan government is wrong, so they
pay under protest. Sadducees believe it should be
paid without reservation.

By answering this question, Jesus will side with
one group or the other. If he says the tax is not
to be paid, Sadducee leaders can report him to
the authorities for teaching treason. If he says to
pay it, Pharisee leaders will refute his message of building a spiritual
kingdom over an earthly kingdom.

> **Come With Me**
> *Your first restorative
> step is toward me.*

They lead in with sweet talk, but their goal is trickery.

Our conversations ought to be genuine, with no hidden layers of false
sincerity. Thankfully, we can always be honest with Jesus, and that's our
first go-to when we don't know what to say. He'll remove the hidden
layers so that we can share what's really on our hearts.

PUSH OUT DEEPER: Luke 20:20–22; Matthew 5:37; Psalm 15:2; James 5:12

Honor the King

> "Well then," he said, "give to Caesar what belongs to Caesar, and give to God what belongs to God."
>
> LUKE 20:25 NLT

THE ACTUAL QUESTION is one of loyalty: Should a Jew be loyal to the government or loyal to God?

His answer is *both*. Give to the king what is his, but give the King of Kings what is due as well.

One king requires a levy. The other King requests reverence and relationship.

One rules. Another redeems.

One is distant. One broke down every wall between man and God.

One offers services. One came to serve.

The Greek word Jesus used in his answer is often translated as "give back." We give our government what is due, for we are beneficiaries. We pray for our government and those in leadership, for that's what God asks us to do.

Yet let us not fail to give back to our King of Kings what is fitting. He is worthy of adoration, so we worship him with our hearts, souls, and minds. He came as a servant, so in turn we serve him, but also widows, orphans, and the fatherless.

He loved us first, so we love him back with all that we are.

Come With Me

Pray for those in authority to have wisdom and discernment, and that I might be in the midst of your nation.

PUSH OUT DEEPER: Luke 20:23–26; Mark 12:30; 1 Timothy 2:1–2; Romans 13:1

Afterlife

"Even Moses showed in the passage about the bush that the dead
come back to life. He says that the Lord is the God of Abraham,
Isaac, and Jacob."

LUKE 20:37 GW

SADDUCEES DO NOT BELIEVE in life after death. Though they
ignore much of the prophets' teaching, they cherish the teaching
and story of Moses.

They tell a story, one that they hope will con-
found Jesus.

A woman is married and has no children, and
her husband dies. In Moses's teaching, that woman
is to marry her deceased husband's brother, so that
she will be protected by family. In their example,
this happens seven times, and in each situation no
child is born. Then they ask, *Who is her husband in the afterlife?*

> ### Come With Me
> *It's difficult to
> comprehend what it
> means for me to be
> your God. In heaven
> you'll know fully!*

It's a farfetched story, yet Jesus listens intently. Then he answers their
true question, which is about the afterlife. He carefully points to Moses's
own words. We will be reunited with God. Heaven is real.

We may have questions about heaven, and there is much to explore,
but we can trust that one day we'll be reunited not only with our loved
ones, but with God himself. There will be great rejoicing, for they'll have
discovered what we could not put into words—the awe we experience
when we worship him face-to-face for the first time.

PUSH OUT DEEPER: Luke 20:27–37; John 14:2–4;
Revelation 7:16–17; Revelation 21:4

208

We Live!

"Now he is not God of the dead, but of the living, for all live to him."

LUKE 20:38 ESV

THE RELATIONSHIP BETWEEN God and his children does not fade when a person dies. They still live, as does the closeness between a heavenly Father and his children.

What a glorious revelation!

Our faith lives brightly while we go about our everyday lives. It's not stagnant. We live and move and breathe in him. That connection only burns brighter after we pass from earth to eternity.

When we breathe our last, we pull in new air, crystal clear.

We close our eyes, only to open them to splendor.

We say good-bye, only to say hello to the One who loves us best.

Our time on earth is but a shadow of what awaits those who call themselves sons and daughters of God.

We live!

> ### Come With Me
> *Your brief time on earth cannot compare with what awaits you in eternity.*

Savior, we often act as if our time on earth will go on forever. It's because we are human. Thank you that we don't have to fear death, not for ourselves, nor for our loved ones who know you. Thank you that glory waits for us. Thank you that our loved ones who are already with you are experiencing that glory even now.

PUSH OUT DEEPER: Luke 20:38–40; Revelation 22:1; Psalm 73:25; Revelation 22:5

Who Am I?

"David calls him 'Lord.' How then can he be his son?"

LUKE 20:44 NIV

FAMILY LINEAGE IS RECORDED and shared from generation to generation, so scribes can easily draw the lineage from David to Mary, the young virgin who became Jesus' mother.

They have also studied and memorized the stories of King David. In his own words, David spoke of the long-awaited Messiah as his Lord. He stated the Messiah would come long after his death.

If Jesus is the Messiah, then he is David's Lord. He is also the Lord of the scribes. But if he is merely Jesus, the son of a carpenter, he is only David's ancestor—a mere man. This puts the scribes at a crossroads. *Who is Jesus?*

> **Come With Me**
> *Who do you say that I am?*

Even in Jesus' last remaining days, he attempts to draw the religious men out of blindness. He came to earth to rescue them, just as he did for others.

For all of us, there comes a moment when we decide who Jesus is. It's a personal one-to-one moment when we ask ourselves these questions:

Is he the Lord of my life? Is this more than just attending church? Is he powerful? Is he all knowing? Does he reach for me? Am I reaching back?

If the answers to these questions are not what we hope, we aren't stuck in that crossroads. We press into Jesus until our head knowledge (what we know about Jesus) becomes heart knowledge.

PUSH OUT DEEPER: Luke 20:41–44; Psalm 110:1; Psalm 145:17–18; Isaiah 55:6

Be Careful

"Beware of the experts in Moses' Teachings! They like to walk around in long robes and love to be greeted in the marketplaces, to have the front seats in the synagogues and the places of honor at dinners."

LUKE 20:46 GW

LIKE AN X RAY, Jesus penetrates to the underlying cravings of the scribes. They like to walk around in long robes because this outerwear designates them as important. They love to be greeted in the marketplace because it feeds their egos. They expect to be seated in the front row in the synagogue and escorted into seats of honor at dinners because they love, love, love the attention.

Jesus exposes their hearts, and it's not pretty. These same men devoured widows' houses by extracting interest on their giving. Even as they pray long prayers, they have missed the heart of God by a mile.

Beware. Be careful. Don't do what they do.

Better to be cloaked in humility than in pride. Better to be unnoticed than greeted out of fear or false appreciation. Better to sit in the back row than expect to always be first.

Better to pray a short prayer in private and hear the encouragement of our Savior than to say a lot when we are the only one listening.

Beware. Be careful. Don't do what they do.

> **Come With Me**
>
> *If you see a flaw in another, ask me to reveal if that same flaw resides in your own heart.*

PUSH OUT DEEPER: Luke 20:45–47; Philippians 2:3; Galatians 5:13; 1 Peter 5:5

Our Not Enough

As Jesus looked up, he saw the rich putting their gifts into the temple treasury.

LUKE 21:1 NIV

A PARADE OF SORTS is in progress. People walk by and pour their offerings into collection boxes. Rich men with brimming purses give a *lot* of money. It looks impressive, but it's not generous.

It's their extra. It's what is left over.

Jesus notices the woman standing in their shadow. She clutches her widow's mite. She's the poorest of the poor. When she arrives at the coffers, she puts in two copper coins equaling almost nothing. It's all she has.

The rich give out of their abundance, but she gives out of her *not enough*.

Jesus is openly pleased by this sacrifice and her love for God behind it.

There are days we don't feel we have enough to give. We don't have enough faith. We don't have enough money. We don't have enough time.

Yet when we give anyway, he notices. He doesn't compare us with the person standing next to us, but sees the sacrifice as we give our *not enough*. As we give what we have, it delights the heart of God. He takes our *not enough*, and it becomes more than enough in his hands.

> ## Come With Me
> *Bring what you have right now—all your doubts, all your faith, all your hope, all your talent, all of you. I see the sacrifice in that, and it's beautiful.*

PUSH OUT DEEPER: Luke 21:1–4; Mark 12:44; 1 Timothy 6:18–19; Psalm 34:15

More Than a Building

"As for these things that you see, the days will come when there will not be left here one stone upon another that will not be thrown down."

LUKE 21:6 ESV

I T'S THE END of the third day of Jesus' last week. The relentless questioning has finally subsided. As Jesus and the disciples leave to find a place to sleep, they draw Jesus' attention to the temple. The white marble walls are a masterpiece. They are adorned with massive jeweled stones. A golden vine, gifted by Herod, drapes in artistic glory across the top. The temple spans across nearly one-sixth of the city.

It's a sight to behold.

As striking as it may be, it's only a building. Forty years later it will be demolished. Not one gigantic stone will be left standing upon another. Though the temple is picturesque, only the Spirit of God can make it truly beautiful. Only the Spirit of God will remain once it is battered and torn down.

We are the church.

It is made up of all races, all nations, all ages.

We may not be beautiful to the eye, and at times we may be battered. When we burst with his presence, however, it will draw the world to Jesus. It's what will last!

Lord, fill up your church with your presence.

> ### Come With Me
> *Pray for revival for my church, and that it will begin with you.*

PUSH OUT DEEPER: Luke 21:5–6; 1 Corinthians 12:27; Proverbs 8:19; Isaiah 33:6

Believe

> And they asked him, "Teacher, when will these things be, and
> what will be the sign when these things are about to take place?"
>
> LUKE 21:7 ESV

IT SEEMS INCREDIBLE that this ragged band of followers has walked closely with Jesus for three years and still struggles with unbelief. From the beginning, Jesus has turned all of their former beliefs upside down.

When Jesus declares the temple will be destroyed, it doesn't seem likely. The building blocks are larger than chariots. The temple is a jewel of architecture and a cornerstone of religion, and surely protected. Still, when Jesus declares its demise one day, the disciples simply ask, "When?" They believe!

They now understand Jesus *is* the Messiah, and if anyone can see the future, it's him. When he speaks the impossible, they immediately look for it to come true. They have transitioned from uncertainty to conviction.

> ### Come With Me
> *You may not be able to see the future, but I know what is ahead. You can place your confidence in me day by day.*

When God speaks and we can't see the end results, we may question it. That's a natural response, for we see the obstacles. We see the impossibility of it all.

Yet our faith isn't grounded in the natural. It's firmly fixed in Christ. If he speaks it, it's true.

When he leads us to consider the impossible, let's ask him *when* and step into belief.

PUSH OUT DEEPER: Luke 21:7–12; John 12:44; John 14:1; Mark 9:24

Testify

And it shall turn to you for a testimony.

LUKE 21:13 KJV

JAMES, THE BROTHER OF JOHN, will be the first to lose his life to the sword. Others will follow. They will be martyred in various ways. Some disciples, like John and Simon the Zealot, will live years longer than the others. Those additional years will mean more opportunities for persecution.

They will also allow more time to testify to the goodness of Jesus.

Followers of Jesus will face persecution, but they will not be shattered. Rather, they'll be scattered across regions, and their testimony will be planted all over the world.

> ### Come With Me
> I never promised walking with me would be easy, but I do promise you'll be transformed as a result.

Our testimony is the mark of our faith. It's not how long we have lived or what we did, but *who* we walked with.

We'll shout these truths!

We are shaken, but he is near. We experience his love, and he shows us how to love others. We pray and hear his voice. We mourn and he comforts us. We fall and he picks us up. We step into deep waters, and he meets us there every time.

Let's share the stories of his faithfulness. They have the power to reach beyond our lifetime, leading others to begin their own story of walking with Jesus.

PUSH OUT DEEPER: Luke 21:13–17; Hebrews 13:3; Acts 20:24; Romans 8:18

Counted

"But not a hair of your head will perish. Stand firm, and you will win life."

LUKE 21:18–19 NIV

J ESUS MAKES A PROMISE, but it feels conflicting.

No hair on your head will perish.

This isn't possible. There will be danger. There will be harm. Some will be beaten. Some will die.

Jesus completes his thought with the second half of the promise.

Stand firm, and you will win life.

Every hair on the disciples' heads has been counted. Physically they may suffer, but not a hair on their heads will perish, because they'll live forever.

We are not promised a life without struggle, but we are assured that every hair on our head is counted. That seems incredible, doesn't it?

It's only a glimmer of how intimately our heavenly Father knows us.

Even in the most difficult of situations, he's aware of what we feel and what we need. He's not distant, but oh so close.

> ## Come With Me
> *You are not desolate in this difficult place, for I am by and with you.*

We stand firm, and even endure, for the One who has counted every hair on our head is with us and will take us through the difficulty to the other side.

Whether in life or beyond, we have that promise; because of that, we win!

PUSH OUT DEEPER: Luke 21:18–19; Psalm 31:24; Colossians 1:11; Jeremiah 1:18

Look Up!

"Then everyone will see the Son of Man coming on a cloud with power and great glory. So when all these things begin to happen, stand and look up, for your salvation is near!"

LUKE 21:27–28 NLT

I N THE YEAR AD 70 Jerusalem will fall, just as Jesus predicts. Afterward, upheaval will reign for generations. All of the signs point to hardship for the Jews.

There's hope, however.

Regardless of how chaotic their earthly existence might one day be, Jesus vows that he will return. Those who believe—whether alive or temporally asleep—will be swept up with him in the clouds. No war can steal away this assurance. No earthly turmoil can hinder his return.

When there is dire news, our instinct might be to look down or to worry.

Let's look *up*!

Our hope is not diminished due to our circumstances. Our well-being isn't determined by wars or rumors of wars. We look up, and there we find the strength we so desperately need. We look *up* because we find security in this promise—he's coming back for us.

Come With Me
When you feel afraid of what is happening in the world, look up!

PUSH OUT DEEPER: Luke 21:20–28; Daniel 7:13; Revelation 1:7; Mark 13:27

His Words Remain

"The earth and the heavens will disappear, but my words will never disappear."

LUKE 21:33 GW

THE DISCIPLES HAVE LEFT BEHIND much to follow Christ, but they are not immune to Satan's ploys. Jesus reminds them to stay the course and not to be overpowered by temptation or betrayed by personal corruption. He tells them, rather, to turn their hearts to the things of God.

They are no strangers to the turmoil that inhabits the world, nor to the possible danger that awaits them for following Jesus. He is reminding them, and us, of the truth that the day of judgment is inevitable, but those who trust in him can rest assured that even in calamity and destruction, his promises hold true.

In the middle of our fears regarding the situations that surround us, we have God's words to cling to. The gospel warned of these occurrences. Once this earth has passed away, those words will remain. These promises are a hope of his return.

> ### Come With Me
> Give me your worries in prayer. This world and earthly things are temporary, but my Word will give you eternal hope of the glory that awaits.

As we reside in the midst of the darkness of this world, let us continue to seek his truth, follow his example, and pray without ceasing. By doing this, we are living a life worthy of spending eternity with Christ.

PUSH OUT DEEPER: Luke 21:29–33; Isaiah 51:6; Isaiah 49:16; Matthew 24:35

Ready

"Watch therefore, and pray always."

LUKE 21:36 NKJV

A WATCHMAN STUDIES THE NIGHT for signs of unrest. He doesn't slumber when he's on duty. He doesn't allow distractions to take him from his post. When the enemy approaches, the watchman alerts the city. Barricades are put up, and weapons are drawn.

The enemy—who thought he'd catch the city unaware—doesn't win, because the watchman was alert.

> **Come With Me**
> *Rather than retreat,
> defeat the enemy
> in prayer.*

We have an enemy, but as watchmen we don't live in fear of his tactics. Regardless of the fight, we serve a powerful God who hears our prayers. He has equipped us for the battle. When we fall to our knees, all of heaven is alerted on our behalf. When we need shelter, we are barricaded in his strength.

Even when the battle is heavy and our hearts are afraid, we stand firm. We aren't distracted by tactics or in trepidation because of his plans.

We stand alert and ready, calling on his name in prayer.

PUSH OUT DEEPER: Luke 21:34–36; Isaiah 62:6; 1 Thessalonians 5:25; Psalm 50:15

Refuge

Each day Jesus was teaching at the temple, and each evening he went
out to spend the night on the hill called the Mount of Olives, and
all the people came early in the morning to hear him at the temple.

LUKE 21:37–38 NIV

EARLY EVERY MORNING JESUS TEACHES at the temple. At the
end of a long day, he and his friends go up on the Mount of Olives.
Surely there is a room for Jesus in the city, but peace waits on the mountain.

There he sleeps. There he refuels. There he finds quiet.

In our crazy, chaotic days we are buzzed with noise and tasks and demands. We are pulled and tugged at, and our bodies and minds cry for rest.

Where is our Mount of Olives?

We may not have a special day, but we are offered rest in our relationship with Jesus. He's our
refuge! There we find rest for our thoughts. There
we refuel. There we find peace that will sustain
us as we go about our busy day.

Let's leave behind the busyness, shut down the
noise, and settle into the refuge.

> ### Come With Me
> *Your thoughts are
> overloaded and
> overstimulated. Turn
> it all off and let my
> peace take over.*

Father, we are exhausted, and sometimes that fatigue is self-inflicted.
We lie in bed and check one more status or one more message rather than
sleep. We pile on tasks that aren't necessary, and cram in appointments you
didn't ask us to make. Help us to simplify our lives. Help us to respect rest,
as you did. Thank you for a busy life, but thank you also for a balanced life.

PUSH OUT DEEPER: Luke 21:37–38; Isaiah 28:12; Isaiah 32:18; Jeremiah 31:25

We Are Wise

Then Satan entered Judas, called Iscariot, one of the Twelve.

LUKE 22:3 NIV

JUDAS HAS LAUGHED WITH JESUS. He's sat with him and listened to his teaching. He's witnessed every miracle Jesus has ever performed. Though he wrestles with his coarser nature, as we all do, Jesus sees good in this disciple.

The enemy appeals to Judas, planting thoughts of discontent. He knows greed is Judas's battleground. This temptation is a pivotal moment, much like what Jesus encountered in the wilderness. Will Judas fight back with truth, or will he succumb?

When we are tempted, we are not without options.

> ### Come With Me
> *You will recognize lies as you are grounded in my truth.*

Though temptation may seem overwhelming, it is never greater than the power of God. When we are tempted, we are wise to recognize the devil's plotting and push his plans to the side. When the enemy appeals to our weak places, we are wise to ask for help.

When the enemy tempts us to go down the wrong path, we are wise to remember that his goal is never to enrich us, but to destroy.

We are wise to remember that we have been given all we need to overcome.

PUSH OUT DEEPER: Luke 22:1–3; John 12:4–6; 2 Corinthians 2:11; 1 Corinthians 10:13

Where Will We Go?

They were delighted, and they promised to give him money.

LUKE 22:5 NLT

JUDAS ISCARIOT HAS CLOSE FRIENDS who are trustworthy. He can go to John or Peter or Matthew (or any of the disciples) and tell them he's heading in the wrong direction. These men have wrestled with their own shortcomings, and they can help put his feet back where they belong.

Instead, he goes to the men who conspire for Jesus' demise. They are surprised, delighted even, at his appearance in their midst. They promise to give him thirty pieces of silver, a small sum for such a betrayal.

Unknown to them, Judas can still make a U-turn. There is no point where he doesn't have the freedom to say, "This is not who I am!"

Where do we go when tempted?

When we are tempted, we can go to those who will agree with our temptation, or turn to a godly friend. A godly friend can help put it to rest as we talk and pray through the temptation. A godly friend can provide clarity.

> **Come With Me**
> That friend who delights in your temptation is no friend at all.

Temptation only becomes sin once we act upon it, but even then we are proposed a way out. Let us not forget that our closest friend is Jesus.

When we are honest about our sin, he offers forgiveness and a second chance.

PUSH OUT DEEPER: Luke 22:4–6; Matthew 26:15; Matthew 6:13; 2 Timothy 4:17

Family

Jesus sent Peter and John and told them, "Go, prepare the Passover lamb for us to eat."

LUKE 22:8 GW

THE PASSOVER FEAST is a family feast, yet here stands a group of men far from their earthly families. Jesus sends Peter and John to a nearby city street. When they see a man carrying a jug of water, he instructs them to follow the man to his home. They'll lodge in the upper guest chamber of that home, where they'll partake of the Passover feast one last time as friends.

Family is often defined as those with whom we are related, but what do we do when our earthly families are far away or broken?

We have the power to choose our closest community.

They may not be related, but we *become* family as we gather together.

We *become* family as we worship, pray, and dig deeper into the Word together.

We *become* family as we show up in the hard places and celebrate in the good.

We *become* family as we urge each other on in our strengths and stand strong together in the gaps.

Come With Me
Do you see that one who needs a family? Show them they aren't alone.

PUSH OUT DEEPER: Luke 22:7–11; Hebrews 10:24–25; Psalm 133:1; Acts 1:14

Remembrance

And he took bread, and when he had given thanks, he broke it and gave it to them, saying, "This is my body, which is given for you. Do this in remembrance of me."

LUKE 22:19 ESV

JESUS HOLDS UNLEAVENED BREAD in his hands, breaks it, and passes it to the disciples.

This is my body, which is given for you.

These words will come to life soon, and they will haunt these men.

If they knew what Jesus was really saying, they might have tried to convince him otherwise. Except it wouldn't have altered the events. When Jesus chose the cross, he did so with these men on his heart. He knew their every flaw. He knew their every sin. He loved them regardless.

The broken bread of communion represents Jesus' body, yes.

It is also a reminder of broken lives mended and liberated on that rugged tree. We were wrecked in our sin, but repaired by his sacrifice. We were lost and without hope, but found. As we take the bread, we remember a Savior who saw our brokenness and put us back together again.

> ## Come With Me
> *The cross heals your sin, but also the wounds from those who sinned against you.*

PUSH OUT DEEPER: Luke 22:12–20; Romans 6:4–6; 1 Corinthians 1:18; Galatians 6:14

A Good Guy

The disciples began to ask each other which of them would ever do such a thing.

LUKE 22:23 NLT

WHEN JESUS SAYS that one will betray him, the disciples are puzzled. They look around the table at the men who have been their constant companions for the past three years. None of them point to Judas Iscariot and say, "It's him! I knew it!"

Judas has learned the art of disguising his real self.

He was chosen because Jesus saw good in him. Jesus also understood Judas's weaknesses. All of the disciples had them, but there was room to grow as they followed Jesus.

Judas didn't grow. He fed his weakness. Greed led to discontent, which led to thievery, which led to deceit, which led to destruction.

> **Come With Me**
> *Don't let that sin fester.*
> *Expose it to the Light.*

There were exits all along this road. Even as Jesus spoke, Judas could have asked his brothers to pray for him. Instead of kissing his Savior in betrayal, he could have kissed Jesus and asked for help.

Hidden sin is destructive. We aren't required to fix it ourselves, to battle alone. Bring it into the light. Tell a godly friend. Ask for accountability and prayer. Don't play the good guy on the outside, but ask for God's goodness in your weakest moments. When we expose hidden sin, we take an exit from a path of destruction to find our real self all over again.

PUSH OUT DEEPER: Luke 22:21–23; John 13:26; John 12:5; 1 John 2:1

Lover of Quarrels

Now a dispute also arose among them as to which of them was regarded to be the greatest.

LUKE 22:24 AMP

THERE'S NEVER A PERFECT TIME for a quarrel, but this is among the worst. Friends have just broken bread together. They've dipped from the same cup. It's a solemn occasion, and Jesus is grieving. He's just revealed that one of those who he loves will betray him.

Their argument is contentious. Hot-blooded. Prickly. Combative.

Their argument is selfish and self-seeking.

What does Jesus think as his friends *choose* to quarrel?

Quarrels arise. We won't always see eye to eye. Some will rub us the wrong way. Perhaps our ill motives cause contention. We are not powerless in those arguments.

> **Come With Me**
> *Quarreling only makes you sad and angry. Pray for a wise response.*

Who's in the room with us? It's Jesus.

Let's abandon our need to be right. We don't have to have the last word. We can share our thoughts without asserting our authority.

Our need to win subsides as we realize the greatest need is Jesus.

PUSH OUT DEEPER: Luke 22:24–26; Proverbs 17:14; Proverbs 20:3; Genesis 13:8

Stand by Me

"You have stayed with me in my time of trial."

LUKE 22:28 NLT

I T'S NOT THE DISCIPLES' FINEST HOUR. They argue bitterly, wrestling for a place of superiority. Shame and reproof are their just deserts, but Jesus gives them a compliment.

You've stayed with me.

Jesus' earthly stay has been lonely. He was different from his siblings. He's different from other religious teachers. His character stands heads above other men, which only marks him for those who want to knock him low.

> ### Come With Me
> *Your loyalty to me is not unnoticed.*

They sometimes act like knuckleheads, but their loyalty is not ignored. It brings him comfort, especially as his death approaches.

When the disciples argue among themselves, Jesus chooses to stand by them—even when they don't deserve it.

Jesus stands by us, and that we cannot refute. He is with us when we mess up, and he's with us when we come to our senses.

We stay with him when we call his name sacred, even as others ridicule faith. We stand by him when we choose conviction over an easy way out. We stand by him as we choose his way, though others don't agree.

Our relationship with Jesus is mutual. He stands by us, always and forever. We gladly stand by him, because we cannot imagine any other way.

PUSH OUT DEEPER: Luke 22:27–31; Proverbs 20:6; Matthew 16:16–17; 2 Peter 1:16

When You Recover

> "But I have prayed for you, Simon, that your faith will not fail. So
> when you recover, strengthen the other disciples."
>
> LUKE 22:32 GW

SATAN ASKED PERMISSION to sift all the disciples like wheat. This winnowing process separates chaff from the kernels of wheat. In Jesus' last hours, the enemy is on the prowl.

Though all of the disciples are targeted, it is Peter who receives Jesus' attention. He knows Peter will betray him—not once, but three times.

Jesus is praying for him.

Peter *will* fail, but his prayer is that Peter's faith will not fail.

That's an important distinction.

We will fail. Even with our best intentions, we mess up. We lose our temper. We say the wrong thing to a loved one. We sin in anger. We gossip, and then want to take it back.

> **Come With Me**
>
> *Every time you get back up from a fall, you are stronger.*

Satan has asked to sift us all like wheat. He loses when we fail but still recover. He loses when we learn from our mistakes. He loses when we help others currently struggling with sin that once tripped us up.

Jesus is praying for us. He believes in us!

We might fall, but our faith will never fail us.

PUSH OUT DEEPER: Luke 22:32–34; James 3:2; Ephesians 4:13; John 1:16

A Sword

And when he came to the place, he said to them, "Pray that you may not enter into temptation."

LUKE 22:40 ESV

THEY ARE IN OLIVET, the place they've stayed each night for the past few days. Rather than sleep, Jesus takes them aside to prepare them. Where he once instructed the disciples to carry no money or provisions, he tells them to gather those items and carry them with them. If any is in need of a sword, he is to sell his cloak in order to buy one.

In just a few hours, they'll need it. They'll also need one more tool: prayer. They'll battle fear just as surely as they battle Roman soldiers. They'll fight against discouragement just as much as they will hunger.

Prayer will be their greatest offense, their most powerful provision.

> **Come With Me**
> *Prayer is more than words. It's a direct link to your heavenly Father.*

When we feel dark times coming, we fill the storehouse. We make certain there's food. We lock the doors and batten down the hatches. We check out our bank accounts. We pull our loved ones close. These are all good things, but we cannot omit the power of prayer.

In uncertain times, it's our greatest weapon. It's our sword! We plan and we prepare, but first we pray.

PUSH OUT DEEPER: Luke 22:35–41; 1 Chronicles 5:20; Philippians 4:6–7; 1 Kings 8:28

A Cupful

"Father, if it is your will, take this cup of suffering away from me. However, your will must be done, not mine."

LUKE 22:42 GW

JESUS KNEELS IN THE GARDEN of Gethsemane while the disciples keep watch nearby. He's in agony. So much so that his sweat is like drops of blood. He's utterly alone with his Father, but not lonely in his hour of anguish.

He prays that the cup of suffering be removed, if it's God's will. In response, he receives nourishment from the cup of his father's love. The only place to kneel is on the ground, but it's where the angels find him and strengthen him.

It's a bleak image, yet beautiful. Jesus received from God what man could not possibly give him. Even in his agony, he found community with his Abba Father.

> ### Come With Me
> It's dark, but you are not alone in this bleak place. Take my cup and let me strengthen you.

A cup of suffering forces us to our knees, for there's no other hope but God. We call out his name, and he holds a cup to our lips as we drink deeply. It's enough nourishment to take us through the next few minutes, the next few hours, the next few days.

Sip by sip, we commune with God.

It's a hard place, but it's beautiful.

Even in the darkness, we are not lonely.

PUSH OUT DEEPER: Luke 22:42–44; Zechariah 10:12; 1 Corinthians 10:16; Psalm 116:13

Keep Watch

> When he rose from prayer and went back to the disciples, he found them asleep, exhausted from sorrow.
>
> LUKE 22:45 NIV

JESUS ASKS HIS FRIENDS to come with him to the garden of Gethsemane. Some are at a distance, while James, John, and Peter settle under a tree to keep watch and pray. These three hear Jesus call out to God. His grief cannot be ignored. Whether they see the angel minister to Jesus, we don't know, but their sorrow is heavy.

So is their fatigue.

Perhaps they pray. Perhaps they long to go closer to Jesus. Eventually they collapse under the weight of sorrow and sleep.

> **Come With Me**
> *Keep watch as you remain near to me.*

They were charged to keep watch. They should have kept their eyes open. They should have alerted Jesus to Judas's approach, but their humanity is exposed in the garden.

Aren't we just as human?

We are asked to keep watch and pray. When our world seems chaotic, we are weary. We stay as close to Jesus as we can, but fatigue threatens.

He's not asking us to repair what is wrong; he's just asking that we stay as close to him as we can.

PUSH OUT DEEPER: Luke 22:45–48; Matthew 25:13; 1 Thessalonians 5:6; Mark 13:36

Put Down the Sword

Jesus said, "No more of this!" And he touched his ear and healed him.

LUKE 22:51 ESV

FEET STAMP AND SWORDS CLASH as disciples leap to Jesus' defense. With a swish, Peter slices an ear from a soldier's head.

Jesus shouts and puts an end to the skirmish. He touches the soldier and restores the ear. His enemies far outnumber his friends in the garden, but Jesus doesn't permit chaos, even when it might benefit him.

Surely there are moments when our heavenly Father is saying, "Stop."

Even as Christians, we engage in chaos because we believe we are right and someone else is obviously wrong.

If we follow Jesus' example, he asks us to do the opposite.

We may not have an opportunity to place a hand over the ear of a soldier, but we can introduce peace into chaos.

> **Come With Me**
>
> *Ask me when to speak and for the words to say. Put your sword away.*

That takes place as we withhold our words and spend them in prayer. That happens as we listen and try to figure out how someone arrived at an opinion before we engage in a debate. Our words are a measure of wisdom and grace mixed in with truth.

When we draw our swords, does that really change anything?

It's not always to our benefit to take a road to peace, but it's who we are as his followers.

PUSH OUT DEEPER: Luke 22:49–51; Ephesians 6:17; Zechariah 4:6; 2 Chronicles 32:8

Regret

> The Lord turned and looked straight at Peter. Then Peter remembered the word the Lord had spoken to him: "Before the rooster crows today, you will disown me three times." And he went outside and wept bitterly.
>
> LUKE 22:61–62 NIV

MANY OF THOSE WHO SUPPORTED Jesus have fled in fear. The fire crackles and Peter warms his hands, though his insides tremble like it's winter. *What is happening?*

Some of Jesus' words tumble into Peter's brain. Jesus had talked about this day, but it didn't quite soak in. Peter didn't know it would be like this. A servant girl who stands around the fire with him recognizes Peter as a Christ follower.

He hears his own words—words that betray Jesus. Not once. Not twice. Three times. That's when he notices Jesus' eyes on him, when Jesus' words come back to him. Jesus said Peter would betray him, but Peter emphatically denied it. In what is one of the saddest days of his life, Peter flees, weeping bitterly.

> ### Come With Me
> *Failure can be the end or your new beginning.*

Failure offers two options: stay down or get back up.

Getting back up is hard, but it's far better than remaining mired in our mistakes. Jesus knew Peter would be restored, even used mightily of God. When we fail completely, complete restoration is available—as we get back up.

PUSH OUT DEEPER: Luke 22:52–62; Romans 11:11–12; Jeremiah 3:22; 1 Samuel 7:3

It Begins

"Tell us, are you the Messiah?" Jesus said to them, "If I tell you, you won't believe me."

LUKE 22:67 GW

AT DAYBREAK, after Jesus' arrest, he is taken to the palace of Caiaphas and the mock trial begins. It's a hasty meeting. It's unlawful. They have a right to gather, but no right to judge Jesus in this manner. They question. They taunt.

Jesus is drained. He has had no sleep.

They find him guilty, but it is their guilty hearts that are black with power. They pepper him with two questions: Are you the Christ? Are you the son of God?

> **Come With Me**
> *Am I the Lord
> of your life?*

If I tell you, you won't believe me. From this time on, the Son of Man will sit at the right hand of the Father.

No matter what Jesus might say, they have already made up their minds. Their unbelief isn't great enough to stop God's plan.

In fact, their refusal to believe only confirms the need for a Savior.

Jesus is the Son of God, and there's nothing we can say or do to diminish that fact. The real question becomes "Will we make him Lord of our own lives?"

We confess that he is Jesus, our Savior.

When we answer with certainty that he is *Lord* of our lives, that's when God's plan begins to unfold for each of us.

PUSH OUT DEEPER: Luke 22:63–71; Romans 10:10; Jude 1:25; Philippians 3:20

Half-Truths

And they began to accuse him, saying, "We found this man misleading our nation and forbidding us to give tribute to Caesar, and saying that he himself is Christ, a king."

LUKE 23:2 ESV

IF THEY ACCUSE HIM OF BLASPHEMY, the charge won't stick. Many have claimed to be the Messiah. So they appeal to Pilate's fear of an uprising. They appeal to his insecurity as a leader.

The religious leaders draw on half-truths to prove their point.

Did Jesus say these things? Yes and no. All of their points come from conversations they instigated, twisting and turning their words to deceive Jesus. It hadn't worked, not once. So they twist his answers one more time.

Jesus *is* truth.

There's no lie to be found in him.

Half-truths are as destructive as full-blown lies. The intent in a half-truth is self-protection or to tarnish the reputation of someone else. Too many will latch on to a half-truth without investigating deeper.

> ### Come With Me
> *Speaking truth begins by being honest with yourself about your motive.*

They believe them, they repeat them, and the damage is done.

Let our yes be yes. Let our no be no.

Better to speak the truth than to disguise our real intent in half-truths and lies.

PUSH OUT DEEPER: Luke 23:1–2; Exodus 23:7; Leviticus 19:11; Psalm 119:29

Not My Problem

When they said that he was [a Galilean], Pilate sent him to Herod Antipas, because Galilee was under Herod's jurisdiction, and Herod happened to be in Jerusalem at the time.

LUKE 23:7 NLT

PILATE DOESN'T BELIEVE JESUS IS GUILTY, so why not set him free? He fears what people will say. Some of the most powerful leaders stand before him. They're outraged. He clearly understands they are trampling laws, but he doesn't call them on it.

The loophole is the fact that Jesus is Galilean. Pilate can pass his pressing problem on to the next guy without backfire. He washes his hands of Jesus for the first time. There'll be another opportunity around the corner.

Spiritual maturity involves taking responsibility, even when we don't want it. When we pass on our problems, seeking loopholes and an easy way out, we might miss what God is trying to teach us. We learn to trust in difficult seasons. We problem-solve with his help. That skill can help us now and in the future.

> **Come With Me**
>
> *Every time we walk through a problem together, you grow in endurance, wisdom, and maturity!*

Thank goodness not every problem is ours to solve.

Some are, however.

Rather than see them as someone else's problems, what might happen if we see them as a growth opportunity?

PUSH OUT DEEPER: Luke 23:3–7; Hebrews 6:1; 1 Corinthians 2:5–6; 1 Corinthians 3:1

Entertain Me

> Herod was delighted at the opportunity to see Jesus, because he
> had heard about him and had been hoping for a long time to see
> him perform a miracle.
>
> LUKE 23:8 NLT

HEROD HEARS THAT JESUS is coming to see him. He hopes for a magic trick or two, or a miracle of magnitude. He wants Jesus to entertain him.

It's not the first time Herod has sought entertainment. He was glad to speak to John the Baptist, a man who ate locusts and honey and wore clothing of camel hair. Eventually, Herod was responsible for John's death—all because he longed to be entertained.

Every question Herod asks Jesus is met with silence. Herod throws up his hands in frustration. He dresses Jesus in royal robes and mocks the King of Kings. He'll find entertainment, even if he has to provide it himself.

> **Come With Me**
> *I will never perform for you, but I will reveal myself to you.*

Jesus didn't give him what he wanted, because it wasn't what Herod needed. Herod needed a life change, not a magic trick.

It's sobering to think we might see Jesus in the same way.

We put him to the side until we need a miracle. We pull out our faith and demand a performance. When he doesn't give us what we want, we wonder if he's God at all. In those times, he hears our prayers. He loves us. His answers might not be what we want, but he gives us what we need.

PUSH OUT DEEPER: Luke 23:8–11; Matthew 14:6–8; Hebrews 12:28–29; 1 Samuel 12:24

Fast Friends

That day Herod and Pilate became friends—before this they had been enemies.

LUKE 23:12 NIV

HEROD AND PILATE ARE LONGTIME ENEMIES, yet the arrest of Christ brings them together. Herod is pleased that Pilate has sent Jesus his way. It appeals to his ego, but it also puts the man he's wanted to see in his court. Pilate is flattered by Herod's appreciation. He's also grateful that he doesn't have to deal with Jesus or the angry priests.

The priests don't like Herod.

Herod doesn't like the priests.

Pilate and Herod have a long history of enmity.

They all come together with the cause of wounding Christ.

It's a fast friendship; it's also fragile.

Jesus is our friend and demonstrates what that looks like. True friendship doesn't look for the benefits; it wants the best for the other. Our faith is the guiding hand in how we nurture or handle a friendship.

We are human and bring flaws into any relationship, but when the core is wrapped around Jesus, it's far from fragile.

> **Come With Me**
> *Do something for a friend today with no other reason but encouragement.*

PUSH OUT DEEPER: Luke 23:12; Proverbs 27:6; Proverbs 18:24; John 15:15

One Voice

"Therefore I will punish Him [to teach Him a lesson] and release Him." [Now he was obligated to release to them one prisoner at the Feast.]

LUKE 23:16–17 AMP

PILATE HAS JUST DECLARED that Jesus is absolutely innocent, but in the next breath he promises to teach him a lesson. He'll scourge Jesus, a terrible flogging that rips the skin to the bone. Jesus has been disgraced and unjustly accused, and Pilate hopes this chastisement will satisfy the unruly crowd.

Chastising Jesus is a coward's way out.

By accepting it, the crowd is complicit in this cowardice.

If only one had stood up to say, "This is wrong!"

It takes only one voice to speak out when something is clearly unfair or unjust. It takes only one voice to make the innocent feel as if they've been heard.

> **Come With Me**
> *One brave word may spur another to courage.*

Every major revival begins with one brave voice.

We may think one voice will never be heard in the fray, but one voice is all it takes to start a movement.

PUSH OUT DEEPER: Luke 23:13–18; Isaiah 53:5; Deuteronomy 25:3; Proverbs 31:8

Two Men

But they kept shouting, "Crucify him! Crucify him!"

LUKE 23:21 NIV

BARABBAS IS IN CHAINS because he killed a man and plundered a city, and was charged as a robber and murderer. His criminal activity is far greater than Jesus' trumped-up charges.

It's customary to release one prisoner during the Feast of the Passover. Pilate throws out two options, Barabbas or Jesus, believing the mob will choose Jesus. The mob's immediate cry is "Crucify him!"

The wrong man is released that day, and the one who came to set us free is taken into custody.

Jesus came in peace, while Barabbas stirred up discord and shed innocent blood. Barabbas was a thief, while Jesus hung between two thieves and shed his blood for the sins of the world.

When we take our eyes off the mob, we see Jesus. It's in this moment that no one would question him if he called ten thousand angels to rescue him. Instead, he looks over the seething mob and sees the raging impact of sin upon the world. The mob is as lost as they can be, even cloaked in their religion.

> **Come With Me**
> It will be harder and harder to choose me, but know that I choose you—always.

How great the love of a Savior who chose to love those who betrayed him. When we are offered the world, let's never forget that Jesus offered himself.

PUSH OUT DEEPER: Luke 23:19–21; Acts 13:28; Joshua 24:15; John 15:19

Prevail

A third time Pilate spoke to them. He asked, "Why? What has he done wrong? I haven't found this man deserving of the death penalty. So I'm going to have him whipped and set free."

LUKE 23:22 GW

SIMILAR TO A GAME OF TUG-OF-WAR, Pilate wrestles with the mob. The crowd's decision is driven by rage.

Once they settle down, they'll come to their senses—or so he reasons. It doesn't happen. They contradict. They shout. They demand their way. Though Pilate is the one with all the power, they eventually overpower him.

In a gross injustice, he crumbles.

Standing firm in our convictions won't come without resistance. Our enemy will attempt to wear down our defenses. We know what is right. We know what is fair. Our convictions are genuine, but there will be times the assault feels great.

> **Come With Me**
>
> *Better to hold your tongue and pray than to have an argument that goes in circles.*

Standing firm isn't what we do or say; it's what we stand on.

Our beliefs are birthed and nurtured as we follow Jesus. When he leads against the grain, he's right there in front of us, showing us where to go and what to do.

When the enemy shouts out, we come closer to Jesus.

PUSH OUT DEEPER: Luke 23:22–24; 2 Chronicles 20:17; Romans 8:36–37; Colossians 2:15

About This Man

As the soldiers led him away, they seized Simon from Cyrene, who was on his way in from the country, and put the cross on him and made him carry it behind Jesus.

LUKE 23:26 NIV

JESUS' KNEES BUCKLE under the beam's weight as he stumbles down the street. Women follow, mourning loudly at the injustice. Soldiers seize a man from the road. They demand Simon carry the cross for Jesus.

What do we know about this man, Simon from Cyrene?

He's father to Alexander and Rufus. His back is strong, or the soldiers wouldn't have plucked him from the crowd. He didn't ask to carry Jesus' cross, but for a moment he offers relief.

> **Come With Me**
> *The cross you carry for my sake will set you free.*

What do we know about this man, Jesus?

His body aches, but his soul is heavier. Even as Simon from Cyrene carries the cross for Jesus, Jesus bears the load of Simon's sins. He suffers physically, but the greater burden is spiritual. The crushing weight of sin has settled upon Jesus.

We are invited to carry a cross. We pick it up when we turn away from sin and turn toward Jesus. We will never bear the weight he did, but what a privilege it is to carry our cross along with him.

PUSH OUT DEEPER: Luke 23:25–27; Mark 15:21; Hebrews 9:26; 1 Peter 2:24

Green Wood

"For if they do these things when the wood is green, what will happen when it is dry?"

LUKE 23:31 ESV

WOMEN WEEP as they trail Jesus on the Via Dolorosa, the road to Golgotha. Jesus turns to face his mourners.

Don't weep for me. Weep for yourselves.

In this last prophecy about the destruction of Jerusalem, his compassion is for the innocent. The religious men who persecute Jesus feel safe in the shadow of the temple, but one day it will fall. Even in his suffering, the women's well-being is on his mind.

> ### Come With Me
> *What do you place your trust in?*

Jesus is green wood.

Green wood burns slowly, while dry wood catches fire with a spark and is consumed in minutes. Rather than pity Jesus, they can place their trust in him. As we imagine Jesus on the road of sorrows, let's not be blind to his power. He consented to his death, for he is green wood and lives forever.

PUSH OUT DEEPER: Luke 23:28–31; Ezekiel 20:47; 2 Corinthians 12:10; 2 Corinthians 13:4

King of the Jews

> When they came to the place called the Skull, they crucified him
> there, along with the criminals—one on his right, the other on
> his left.
>
> LUKE 23:33 NIV

JESUS HANGS BETWEEN TWO THIEVES. His breath is ragged. His brow bleeds from the jagged thorns pressed into his forehead. His clothing lies in a pile at his feet as Roman soldiers throw dice to claim the rags. A soldier presses a sponge dripping with vinegar to his lips.

A sign hangs over his head: King of the Jews.

In the heavenlies, light and darkness clash. Satan's grip on humanity loosens and the enemy looks on in horror.

> **Come With Me**
> *My death was the
> beginning of life for you.*

Sin is seized and its dark power shaken.

The Spirit of the Lord is on me, because he has anointed me to proclaim good news to the poor. He has sent me to proclaim freedom for the prisoners and recovery of sight for the blind, to set the oppressed free, to proclaim the year of the Lord's favor.

He came.

He gave.

He suffered.

He conquered.

He did all of this for us. We are the beneficiaries. Let us not take for granted his mercy. May we cry in gratitude and receive the gift with awe.

PUSH OUT DEEPER: Luke 23:32–38; Luke 4:18–19;
2 Corinthians 5:15; 1 Corinthians 11:24

Never Too Late

And he was saying, "Jesus, [please] remember me when You come into Your kingdom!" Jesus said to him, "I assure you and most solemnly say to you, today you will be with Me in Paradise."

LUKE 23:42–43 AMP

TWO THIEVES HANG on either side of Jesus. One taunts him, claiming that if he were the Messiah, he would save them all from certain death. The other thief begs for mercy and finds it. One uses his last breaths to condemn Jesus, the other to call him Lord. One enters eternity in anguish. The other dies, but finds new life in Paradise.

It's never too late to receive mercy and a new start.

> **Come With Me**
> *My cup of mercy awaits.*

There is no pit so deep, no sin so great, no failure so insurmountable that our Savior can't rescue us—if only we ask.

We don't have to wait until we've accumulated a mountain of regrets.

We can call out for mercy even now.

Let's not wait one more minute to claim his mercy as true.

Jesus, our regrets are many and we've shied away as a result. If we go one more day without receiving your mercy, that's one more regret. Forgive every wrong. Every wasted moment. Make us new again.

PUSH OUT DEEPER: Luke 23:39–43; Romans 10:13; Romans 3:23–24; Romans 8:1

Veiled No More

> By this time it was about noon, and darkness fell across the whole land until three o'clock. The light from the sun was gone. And suddenly, the curtain in the sanctuary of the Temple was torn down the middle.
>
> LUKE 23:44–45 NLT

HIS MOTHER IS AT HIS FEET, WEEPING. His brothers, Jude and James, stand at a distance. John the Beloved is near. Soldiers guard his broken body in order that none will attempt to save him.

Darkness falls over the land. For three hours the sun hides its face. Jesus cries out as a victor, "It is finished!" The veil in the temple—which has separated mankind from the holy of holies for generations—is ripped from top to bottom.

Forevermore, nothing divides God's children from his presence.

Jesus has become the final sacrifice.

The veil in the temple was torn, but other veils were lifted that day. James and Jude acknowledged Jesus' deity. They had questioned him, but now they'll be among those who gather in the upper room.

> **Come With Me**
>
> *Let me remove the veil that keeps you at a distance.*

They'll tell the world that Jesus was—and is—Lord of all.

Jesus' life and his death lifts the veil from our own eyes. He rips away every barrier that dares to stand between ourselves and God. We are no longer separated from him, but washed in his brilliant light.

PUSH OUT DEEPER: Luke 23:44–49; Exodus 26:31–37; Hebrews 9:3–4; Psalm 31:5

Touching Jesus

This man went to Pilate and asked for the body of Jesus. Then he took it down, wrapped it in linen, and laid it in a tomb that was hewn out of the rock, where no one had ever lain before.

LUKE 23:52–53 NKJV

JOSEPH IS A MEMBER OF THE COUNCIL, a respected man about town. He voiced his protest over the unjust treatment of Jesus. By burying Jesus, he braves public opinion.

Taking down the bloodied body makes him unclean in the eyes of the people. He won't be able to participate in the Passover feast.

> ### Come With Me
> *Your sincere worship reaches tenderly to heaven.*

Touching Jesus is more important to Joseph than a religious ritual. He wraps Jesus' body in spotless linen. Jesus is laid in a burial tomb in a garden, and prophecy is fulfilled.

Joseph might pay a price of public opinion, but it is nothing compared with the price Jesus just paid.

We touch Jesus as we push close to him, even as the world requests we pull away. We touch him as we call ourselves his, even when others reject him. We touch Jesus when we remember his sacrifice and commune with him.

Jesus never backed away from touching the sick, the broken, the hurting.

Savior, we reach to touch you with our praise. Thank you for the scars you bear. We lift our hands and worship you.

PUSH OUT DEEPER: Luke 23:50–56; Isaiah 53:9; Luke 7:39; Matthew 8:15

Rolled Away

> They found the stone rolled away from the tomb, but when they entered, they did not find the body of the Lord Jesus.
>
> LUKE 24:2–3 NIV

THE WOMEN ARRIVE at the break of dawn with aromatic spices. They've lost a friend, but they've also lost hope that he would defeat death. The spices, intended for use in preparing the body, are proof of their devotion. It's all they know to do.

A massive rock seals the entrance of the sepulcher. Sentries are on guard to keep anyone from stealing his body, yet the tomb gapes open as they approach.

The rock is rolled away!

A bright light floods the empty tomb, and two men in shining garments sit, one at the head and one at the foot of where Jesus' body once lay.

In absolute amazement, the women run to tell the story.

> **Come With Me**
> *I will breathe life into you and reignite your faith.*

When we are discouraged, our burdens feel too big to roll away on our own. We love God, but we are tired. We hold on because we can't imagine a life without him.

God meets us in the center of our discouragement.

His light floods our tired faith.

Love rolls the stone away, and renewed faith becomes our story.

PUSH OUT DEEPER: Luke 24:1–4; John 20:22; Ezekiel 37:5; Genesis 2:7

Ministering Angels

Then they remembered his words.

LUKE 24:8 NIV

AN ANGEL APPEARED to Mary the day she conceived Jesus and soothed her troubled heart. Angels filled the sky to announce Jesus' birth, telling the shepherds not to be afraid. An angel ministered to Jesus' weary soul in the garden of Gethsemane.

It's not surprising to find angels in the open tomb now.

They remind Mary Magdalene, Joanna, and the others of Jesus' words. As the angels speak Jesus' words, it's as if Jesus is sitting next to them.

They heard his words before, but now they hear them as if for the first time.

Ministering angels are around us, for Scripture says it is so.

Come With Me
You have direct access to your heavenly Father in my name.

Their role is to serve a God of worship, but not to be worshiped. They are messengers, instruments of God, under his authority. They work on his behalf, ministering to his children.

The Bible clearly instructs us not to place them higher than our God. Only God is worthy of worship, and nothing else can take his place.

PUSH OUT DEEPER: Luke 24:5–8; Luke 1:30; Luke 2:9–14; Hebrews 1:14

The Tomb Is Empty

Peter, however, got up and ran to the tomb. Bending over, he saw the strips of linen lying by themselves, and he went away, wondering to himself what had happened.

LUKE 24:12 NIV

DUST SCATTERS as the women run to tell the disciples what they've found. They spill the news about the angels, sharing every word and detail. Peter and John race for the tomb. They don't believe what the women have told them, but rush to the garden just in case it's true.

John would love nothing more than to see his beloved Savior one more time.

Peter is a man in need of redemption. The last time he saw Jesus was when he betrayed him. If Jesus is alive, perhaps he can say he's sorry.

> **Come With Me**
> *When you choose me,*
> *you choose life!*

If Jesus is alive, there's hope.

The tomb *is* empty.

It proves beyond doubt that Christ rose from the dead. He carried the sins of the world to the grave. He conquered death and hades. The empty tomb proves he is the God of all, for only God can conquer death.

PUSH OUT DEEPER: Luke 24:9–12; Acts 3:15; Acts 4:33; 1 Peter 1:3

250

Better Together

> While they were talking, Jesus approached them and began walking with them. Although they saw him, they didn't recognize him.
>
> LUKE 24:15–16 GW

BOTH HAVE WALKED THROUGH the darkness of losing their Master. The two disciples find comfort in one another as they seek to find what they have lost. Though they don't have any answers, there is some peace as they mutually grieve.

Better they walk together on this stretch of their journey than apart.

Jesus walks with us as we struggle to find him in the midst of the madness that often surrounds us. He has given us community with other Christians as a way to feel Him close and stay the course.

> ### Come With Me
> *I care about your struggles, fears, grief. Don't isolate yourself in these feelings. Surround yourself with those who will guide you back to me.*

We are better together. When one grieves, so should another.

When one is struggling to find hope, another points to Jesus.

It is there that our faith is restored in the beautiful creation that is humanity. Relationship and Jesus are found when we allow ourselves to open up one to another.

PUSH OUT DEEPER: Luke 24:13–16; Psalm 133:1; Galatians 6:2; Ephesians 4:16

All the Way

> "We had hoped he was the Messiah who had come to rescue Israel.
> This all happened three days ago."
>
> LUKE 24:21 NLT

TWO BELIEVERS bend their heads together, deep in conversation. They walk the road to Emmaus, seven miles from Jerusalem. It's the wrong direction, for back in Jerusalem an empty tomb has just been discovered. They go over the events of the last three days, comparing stories and trying to unknot the confusing details. Suddenly there's a third in their midst.

He asks what they are discussing.

They explain that Jesus was crucified, and with that their hopes died with him.

Jesus didn't just draw near to these two disappointed followers. He walked the rest of the way with them.

> ## Come With Me
> *The road seems long, but I'm walking every step with you.*

Jesus comes near, that we can trust. In discouragement, he's in our midst. In a long season of waiting, he's right there. When two or three pray together, he's in the middle of those prayers.

Jesus takes the long road, walking with us to the very end.

PUSH OUT DEEPER: Luke 24:17–21; Matthew 18:20; Isaiah 43:2; Jeremiah 17:8

I Want to Believe!

"They said his body was missing, and they had seen angels who told them Jesus is alive!"

LUKE 24:23 NLT

SHIMMERING LIGHT BLANKETED the women as they saw it for themselves. They ran to tell the disciples, and the word spread among the followers of Jesus.

But the women weren't the first to tell the news.

Jesus had told them repeatedly he would suffer, die, and conquer death on the third day. Only now they believe. Only now they understand.

The Word speaks truths to us repeatedly.

Aren't you more valuable than the sparrow?

I have loved you with an everlasting love.

I have a plan for you.

I loved you at your darkest.

We've heard them, more than once, but do we believe?

Open the eyes of our understanding, Father, to receive your Word as truth. Let it sink in and make itself at home in our soul. May it shape our thoughts and influence the way we live.

> ### Come With Me
> *Your utmost adventure is in the Word. Every time you believe, something new takes place inside of you.*

PUSH OUT DEEPER: Luke 24:22–24; Jeremiah 31:3; Romans 5:8; Matthew 10:31

Scripted

Ought not Christ to have suffered these things, and to enter into his glory?

LUKE 24:26 KJV

JESUS APPEARS TO THE TWO DISCIPLES the same day he arose. It is his first public appearance after the resurrection. These men are not in the inner circle. They are far from the hub of activity. If Jesus appeared in Jerusalem instead of on a lonely road to Emmaus, everyone in the city would have known he was alive.

Nothing he did that afternoon was expected, but Jesus never followed a script.

If he had, he wouldn't have chosen suffering.

If he had, he would have scolded the disciples for their lack of belief rather than assuring them.

If he had followed the script of man, he would have abandoned the world that rejected him.

> **Come With Me**
> *Let me write a new chapter of your life today.*

Jesus chose the cross, and by doing so he chose glory. That glory extends to us. It's written on our lives. When we know him, we know his glory. Our faith is not a script. It's written day by day. We listen for his voice, and we respond. We hear him say, "Go this way," and we do. We enter into a glorious relationship with God, a script written long before time and by God himself.

PUSH OUT DEEPER: Luke 24:25–26; Hebrews 2:10; 2 Corinthians 3:17–18; Romans 9:23

Road to Jesus

And their eyes were opened, and they recognized him. And he
vanished from their sight.

LUKE 24:31 ESV

THE HOLY SPIRIT OPENS THEIR EYES, and they recognize him.
Then he vanishes.

Jesus has not ascended, not yet. He has one foot on earth and another
in heaven, but he's definitely alive!

What began as a seven-mile walk filled with disillusionment has
quickly changed into something astonishing. They talked with the Master. They broke bread with him. He asked ques-
tions and listened without judgment.

> ### Come With Me
> *When you encourage
> someone who is
> discouraged, you
> minister to me.*

It's almost too wonderful to believe, and yet
it's true.

When we are on a road to despair, Jesus offers
a detour. It's a perfectly paved road that leads to
hope. That detour may be surprising and unfamil-
iar, yet it's a path of faith. We talk with Jesus as we go. We break bread
with him and tell him how we feel. We may not recognize him and his
actions until we have reached the end of our trip, but it's Jesus!

Despair is a temporary road that fosters dependence on God. His
love is never detoured by our despair. He shows us how to find the exit,
and off we go on an adventure of faith.

PUSH OUT DEEPER: Luke 24:27–31; Matthew 25:35–36; Psalm 43:5; Psalm 94:19

His Presence

> They asked each other, "Were not our hearts burning within us while he talked with us on the road and opened the Scriptures to us?"
>
> LUKE 24:32 NIV

IT'S A LONG SEVEN MILES BACK to their friends, but they cannot wait to get started. As they walk, they go over their conversation with Jesus. They remember the moment Jesus entered the conversation. Their hearts burned! There was nothing new in their conversation except the presence of Jesus.

When Jesus came on the scene, it redirected the conversation entirely.

When we hash out an issue again and again, it becomes old news. It can also become an old wound. We debate it. We toss out opinions. We hold our ground in an argument, even when we are wrong. We turn a conversation upside down, sideways, and inside out. It takes on a life of its own, and soon we don't know which side is up.

What if we bring it to Jesus first?

What if we bring him that cantankerous issue or disappointment? What if we bring him our hurts long before we express them to anyone else? Introducing the presence of Jesus redirects our conversations from old news to revelation.

Father, when we are tempted to talk about these things with everyone else, remind us to come to you first.

> **Come With Me**
>
> *The more you repeat it, the more complex it becomes. Whisper those words to me first.*

PUSH OUT DEEPER: Luke 24:32–35; John 21:23; Colossians 1:9; James 1:26

Jesus Himself

While they were talking about this, Jesus Himself [suddenly] stood among them and said to them, "Peace be to you."

LUKE 24:36 AMP

THE CITY IS STILL in an uproar over the empty tomb, and all who follow Jesus are in danger. The door is tightly bolted, and when the two disciples bang on the door, they are let in. Quickly they throw the bolt back in place.

The followers share their startling news. They saw Jesus on the road to Emmaus!

First, Joanna and Mary Magdalene sighted the angels and the empty tomb. Then Jesus appeared to Simon Peter and forgave him for his betrayal. Now Jesus has been sighted a third time.

Can it be true?

Suddenly Jesus himself stands among them. Terror strikes their hearts, and they fall to the ground in fear. Jesus greets them, and peace floods their hearts. Terror flees as wonder takes its place.

Come With Me
If you are afraid to open the door, I will come to you, wherever you might be.

We may believe the door is shut tight, bolted by fear and discouragement. We wonder if Jesus can make it through. But nothing can keep Jesus away from his own. No valley is so low, no mountaintop so high that his presence is denied.

PUSH OUT DEEPER: Luke 24:36–37; Psalm 23:4; Deuteronomy 20:1; 2 Samuel 22:19

It's Really Me

"Look at my hands. Look at my feet. You can see that it's really me.
Touch me and make sure that I am not a ghost, because ghosts
don't have bodies, as you see that I do."

LUKE 24:39 NLT

JESUS HOLDS OUT HIS HANDS scarred with nail prints. He shows
them his feet.

The evidence is clear.

It's really me.

His followers touch him. They kneel at his feet to examine his scars.
They touch his side where the sword pierced. They dance and shout, for
Jesus is among them.

Jesus will be with them for forty days. He'll
eat with them. He'll show them his glory. He will
reveal a new way to walk with him.

> **Come With Me**
>
> *Every second, every hour,
> every day I am near.*

He'll soon leave, but he doesn't have to be with
them physically to be their friend. As they go
out into the world to spread the gospel, he'll be with them all the way.

We feel his presence strongly many days, and other days we don't.
In each of these, he is right there.

Touch me. It's really me.

We are asked to feel the wound in his side. To run our fingertips over
his nail-scarred hands. We may not see Jesus with our eyes, but our spirit
confirms it is him. He is with us all along the way.

PUSH OUT DEEPER: Luke 24:38–43; Acts 10:33; Ephesians 2:18; Ephesians 3:12

My Mission Is Complete

> Then he said to them, "These are my words that I spoke to you
> while I was still with you, that everything written about me in the
> Law of Moses and the Prophets and the Psalms must be fulfilled."
>
> LUKE 24:44 ESV

THEY GATHER AROUND JESUS in the upper room. He eats a piece
of broiled fish, dining with them one last time. As he speaks to
them, their minds are freed. Every obstacle is removed. It all makes
sense now, every last word.

Jesus has fulfilled the prophecies and the law. His mission is complete.
Theirs is soon to begin.

Jesus will leave them, but his teaching is in them.

He has shown them what to do and equipped them for the job ahead.
There is no more mystery as to Jesus' role, but they have no idea what
their mission will look like. They don't ask for a
map or a written plan, but Jesus will show them
what to do.

Come With Me
*You have a place
in my mission.*

Jesus completed his mission on earth, and
ours began.

Each mission is different because we are differ-
ent. Our goal is to finish the race and complete the task the Lord Jesus
has given us—the task of testifying to the good news of God's grace.

PUSH OUT DEEPER: Luke 24:44–45; Acts 12:24–25; Acts 20:24; 1 Thessalonians 3:2

World Changers

"You are witnesses of all these things."

LUKE 24:48 NLT

THEY HAVE WITNESSED all manner of miracles, from the lame leaping to their feet to blinded eyes opened. They were present when Jesus died, and they witnessed the empty tomb.

They are witnesses, but there is more to see.

Jesus asks them to remain in the upper room to receive a gift of power that will launch them into destiny. He prays over them and releases them to full-time ministry.

The disciples witness one more wonder as Jesus is carried to heaven.

They will become world changers because of their relationship with Jesus.

> **Come With Me**
> There is no such thing as an ordinary life if I'm at the center.

What wonders have we witnessed? That prodigal child returning home. That broken spirit revived. Addictions shattered. Apathy put aside. Wonder restored. Even if we describe our lives as ordinary, we have witnessed extraordinary miracles in our faith.

God takes our lives and assigns purpose. We are world changers because of what we have witnessed, and we cannot help but tell another.

Lord, we've witnessed *you*. Help us become world changers, beginning in our own homes, and wherever else you want to take us.

PUSH OUT DEEPER: Luke 24:46–50; John 15:27; Acts 2:32; Acts 2:42–43

Come With Me

And they worshiped Him and returned to Jerusalem with great joy
[fully understanding that He lives and that He is the Son of God];
and they were continually in the temple blessing and praising God.

LUKE 24:52–53 AMP

I F WE LOOK BACK at where the followers of Christ began, we can see they lived ordinary lives. They were fishermen, farmers, and tax collectors. Some were lost. Others were tormented. Some were positioned in power. Some never gave a thought to changing the world. When they met Jesus, they had no idea where the relationship might lead.

> **Come With Me**
>
> *I have a new chapter to write in your life. Let's go!*

When he said, "Come with me," and they said yes, it transformed them, and history, forever. They were more than converts. They were committed.

They were more than followers. They were devoted.

Come with me.

What a glorious invitation. What a glorious Savior. Oh, worship the Lord almighty who was and is and is to come! Praise him for who he is, and who you are because of him. He lives and is the Son of God! Say yes to his invitation, following wherever he asks you to go, whatever miracle he desires to do in or through you.

Yes, Lord. We say yes!

PUSH OUT DEEPER: Luke 24:51–53; Mark 16:15; 1 Peter 2:9; John 17:9–11

"The Spirit of the Lord is upon me, for he has anointed me to bring Good News to the poor. He has sent me to proclaim that captives will be released, that the blind will see, that the oppressed will be set free, and that the time of the Lord's favor has come."

LUKE 4:18–19 NLT

ACKNOWLEDGMENTS

WRITING A 260-DAY DEVOTIONAL took this writer on a faith journey. There were days I wept as I wrote, overwhelmed with the story of Jesus. There were other days that I prayed for words to come, asking that God fill what seemed to be an empty well.

I'm grateful for my sweet guy who took over the cooking and who served as encouragement on our walks at the end of a long writing day. Richard, you have always been my cheerleader, but you are so much more. Thank you for laying your hands on me and praying on the harder days.

Thank you to my children: Leslie and Stephen, Ryan and Kristin, Melissa and Josh. Thank you for understanding during deadlines and for cheering me on. I love you. Thank you to my "littles," Elle, Luke, Jane, Audrey, Josiah, and Caleb.

I want to thank my editor and friend Kim Bangs. Surely you go far beyond the norm as you champion your writers.

Thank you to the Bethany House team, including Carra Carr and Shaun Tabatt, and every member of the Bethany team whose creativity touched this book. A special thank-you to Natasha Sperling for her gentle editing mixed with encouragement.

Thank you to The FEDD Agency team extraordinaire, who believed in this book from the beginning. Esther, I am grateful for you and your entire team. You define the word *excellence*.

There are many who need to be listed, but there are simply not enough pages.

I'm surrounded and strengthened by friends like Crystal Hornback, my #livingfreetogether group, my gorgeous Wednesday night Bible study friends, and the Proverbs 31 Ministries team. Thank you for your support. There are miles between some of us, but it never feels that way.

Suzanne Eller (Suzie) is the author of hundreds of articles and nine books, including *Come With Me: Discovering the Beauty of Following Where He Leads*. Suzie serves with Proverbs 31 Ministries as a writer for the *Encouragement for Today* daily devotions, and has served as a Bible teacher for the P31 app First5, which reaches over one million women with the Word of God. She also serves on the International Initiative team, partnering with ministries that lift women out of oppression and share the hope of Christ.

She's an international speaker, ministering in several countries and across the United States.

Suzie is a popular radio and TV guest, and has been featured on hundreds of programs, including *Focus on the Family*, *100 Huntley Street*, *Aspiring Women*, K-LOVE, *The Harvest Show*, and many others. She's a regular radio contributor to KLRC 90.9 FM.

Suzie's greatest joy comes from watching women discover the power of God's Word, and seeing his handiwork in their lives. She has developed free Bible study curriculum that are easily accessed and downloaded. Her hope is that these will encourage spiritual growth and maturity for women across the world at no cost. Find out more at www.tsuzanne eller.com.

Suzie and her husband, Richard, live in Northwest Arkansas. She's mom to three grown children and their spouses, and "Gaga" to six beautiful grandchildren. When she's not writing or speaking, she's with the guy she loves, hiking, kayaking, or running after one of their "littles."

Connect With Suzie

www.tsuzanneeller.com
www.facebook.com/SuzanneEllerP31
www.twitter.com/SuzanneEller
www.pinterest.com/SuzieEller
www.proverbs31.org